MW00565332

mob 6

Tasty 6-Ingredient Meals

EBURY
PRESS

Introduction

The aim of this book is simple: we want to prove that you can cook something special – not just a half-decent dinner but a memorable meal your mates will be raving about for years to come – using just 6 ingredients. It might not sound like a lot of ingredients, but that's kind of the point. Cooking doesn't have to be complicated to be delicious.

Every recipe in this book maximises on flavour and provides a fresh, exciting and genuinely innovative example of what you can make from very little. You won't find any precious, overly complex recipes here – just 6 simple ingredients that, when combined correctly, produce some killer dishes. Don't let the simplicity fool you: these recipes are anything but basic. We're talking about dishes that will make your taste buds lose their little minds, like juicy steak with a zesty madras curry butter sauce (page 197), crispy-skinned roast chicken with all the trimmings and a simple garlicky gravy (page 195) and tender pork chops with sweet peaches and fiery padron peppers (page 215).

While using fewer ingredients on the whole means that these recipes are more affordable and accessible than ever, we have occasionally splurged on an ingredient like a big fat steak or a jar of fancy beans because we want to make sure the dish tastes like the best version of itself. We've also used a couple of ingredients that are a tiny bit harder to find – like, for instance, pickled sushi ginger or guindilla chilli peppers – but we've only put them in there because they slap. Don't like an ingredient we've used? Swap it out. No stress. We want you to use these recipes as a guide because, ultimately, you know what you like better than we do, and the whole point of *Mob 6* is to help you enjoy the process of cooking and eating as much as possible.

The truth is, despite what some chefs might tell you, you don't need an ingredients list as long as your forearm to make a delicious meal. Coming up with the recipes for *Mob 6* gave us an opportunity to reassess the way we look at cooking; it's forced us to think more creatively about ingredients and how to get the most out of the basics. Sometimes that means using shallots three ways in one recipe (page 90). Sometimes that means using capers *and* the brine that comes in the jar. Sometimes that means taking thrifty shortcuts like using pre-made pizza dough or shop-bought jam. While we've cut a few corners to help you save time and money, there have been absolutely no compromises when it comes to flavour. We are so, so proud of the tastiness, variety and sheer inventiveness you'll find stuffed in these pages that you're about to delve into. So, go on – get stuck in.

THE RULES

WHAT DOESN'T COUNT IN THE 6

Okay, let's get this out the way before we get endless people writing in about there being more than 6 ingredients in some of these recipes. Yes, there are a very small handful of ingredients that we haven't counted as part of the 6 ingredients. But if that wasn't the case then pretty much every recipe in this book would be for some version of salty, peppery, oily bread – and no one wants that, do they? We hope you already have all of these ingredients in your kitchen cupboard and we hope you understand why we haven't included them in the 6. We're recipe developers, not miracle workers.

Salt
Freshly ground black pepper
Olive oil
Neutral oil (something like vegetable, sunflower, rapeseed oil, etc.)

WHAT DOES COUNT IN THE 6

Literally everything else.

HOW TO GET THE MOST OF YOUR 6

We hope this book inspires you to go out and make your own 6-ingredient inventions. To help you out, here's a bit of a guide on how to think about building the flavour profile of your dishes and getting the best out of your ingredients.

ACIDITY

Is there an ingredient that can cut through the richness and fattiness of what you're making, and really make your dish pop? Think about lemons, limes and vinegar, but also consider the brines that may accompany your olives, capers and pickles. Could different sharp-tasting fruits like pineapple or grapefruit work? How about a tangy spice like sumac? It's even worth considering some dairy like Gorgonzola, yoghurt, buttermilk and Parmesan. There are heaps of acids out there worth exploring.

TEXTURE

When building a dish, it's important to carefully consider the texture and how you can achieve a good balance. A textural contrast on your plate always makes a meal infinitely more enjoyable to eat. The main textures you should consider are crunchy, creamy, chewy, saucy, crumbly and smooth. Of course, not every recipe needs every single texture, but it's great to keep all the options in mind.

We all love a good crunch, right? So think about incorporating crusty bread, shattering pastry, crumbled nuts, crispy onions and chopped veggies like cucumber and carrot into your dish. Could you fry one of the ingredients you've already got until it's crisp and crackly? Get inventive.

DOUBLING UP

There are many ingredients that can be cooked in multiple different ways to make a recipe more exciting to eat.

Onions – These can be eaten raw, pickled, sautéed, caramelised and roasted to bring different flavour profiles to a recipe.
Bread – This could be soft, or toasted and chewy, crisp as croutons or sprinkled on top of a dish as breadcrumbs for extra crunch.
Carrots, courgettes and lots of veg (this applies to crunchy vegetables like broccoli and beetroot) – their flavours and textures can be completely altered whether eaten raw (crisp and fresh) or cooked (sweet and soft).

EMBRACE SHORTCUTS

There are so many products in supermarkets these days that have much of the work already done for us. So, why add more steps, when someone has already gone to the trouble? Some of our favourite shortcuts include:

Ginger garlic paste – A staple jar to have on hand that gives you two ingredients for the price of one.
Pastry – Puff, shortcrust and filo are all readily available and most supermarket versions just so happen to be vegan, too.
Focaccia – Pre-made focaccia can help bring even more flavour to your dishes with a welcome thump of garlic and rosemary.
Pesto – A Mob classic that isn't just for students. You can get truly stellar versions of pesto in the chilled section of the supermarket.
Pickles and ferments – Cornichons, pickles, sushi ginger, kimchi, guindilla chilli peppers and lime pickle all bring a sharpness and complexity to the party that is so important when creating balanced dishes.
Curry pastes – When you're short on time and want to minimise the number of ingredients you're using, curry pastes come to the rescue.

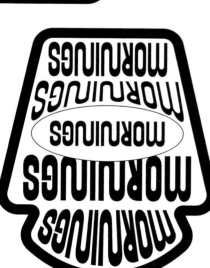

Lime Pickle Halloumi Naan

THE DISH

Lime pickle is such an underrated condiment. It's sharp, spicy and goes great with just about anything. Here, it combines with a gorgeous runny egg to create a riotously rich sauce that brings the whole dish together.

INGREDIENTS

4 tbsp **extra virgin olive oil**
250g pack of **halloumi**, sliced 2cm thick
4 tbsp **lime pickle**
2 **eggs**
2 small **naan**
1 **avocado**, halved, pitted and peeled
a handful of **coriander**, leaves picked, stalks finely chopped
salt and **black pepper**

METHOD

Preheat the grill to a medium-high heat.

Add 2 tablespoons of olive oil to a frying pan and set over a medium heat. Once hot, add the halloumi slices and fry until golden in colour, about 1½ minutes on both sides.

Mix the remaining olive oil with the lime pickle and spoon half over the halloumi slices, toss to coat and push to one side of the pan.

Crack both eggs into the pan and cook until the whites are set, about 2 minutes.

Meanwhile, put the naan onto a baking tray and grill for about 1 minute on each side. Remove from the grill, mash half of the avocado down on each naan with a fork, sprinkle over the coriander stalks and season generously with salt and pepper.

Top with halloumi slices and fried eggs and drizzle over any remaining lime pickle from the pan. Scatter over the coriander leaves to garnish and give the eggs a grind of black pepper (you shouldn't need salt here as the lime pickle is salty enough).

SWAP

If lime pickle's not your jam, try mango chutney instead.

Greens, Eggs + Ham

THE DISH

Dr. Seuss would be chuffed with this brunchy one-pot wonder. When using minimal ingredients, it's not a bad idea to splurge on the best ingredients you can find. Fridge-fresh, shop-bought pesto will make this taste miles better than any jarred versions out there.

INGREDIENTS

2 tbsp **extra virgin olive oil**
2 **courgettes**, sliced thinly into rounds
3 **garlic cloves**, grated or finely chopped
200g **spinach**
4 tbsp **fresh pesto** (check the label if making
    gluten-free)
4 **eggs**
6 slices of **prosciutto**
salt and **black pepper**

METHOD

Heat the olive oil in a frying pan set over a high heat and add the sliced courgettes, frying until golden, about 6 minutes. The courgettes need to get colour, without getting mushy and overcooked, so take care not to stir too much.

Add the garlic and spinach, then pop a lid on to help the leaves wilt, which will take 1–2 minutes. Gently stir through the pesto.

Make 4 wells in the mixture, then crack an egg into each well. Cook for 2–3 minutes until the whites of the eggs are set and the yolks are still runny. Pop the lid on for a bit to help it along.

Tear the prosciutto over the top, season with salt and black pepper and serve.

Blueberry Crumpet Eggy Bread

THE DISH

There's a special place in our hearts for eggy bread. Call it French toast if you're feeling fancy but, either way, this is our kind of comfort food. The crumpet's signature holes are what make it ideal for soaking up the custard and syrup into all of its delicious nooks and crannies.

INGREDIENTS

200g **blueberries**
1 tbsp **maple syrup**, plus extra to drizzle
2 **eggs**
6 tbsp **whole milk**
4 **crumpets**
2 tbsp **vegetable oil**
2 heaped tbsp **crème fraîche**

METHOD

Put the blueberries in a saucepan with the maple syrup and 2 tablespoons of water. Set over a medium heat and bring to a simmer, cooking for 8–10 minutes until the blueberries are soft and have released a purply syrup.

Meanwhile, whisk together the eggs and milk in a large bowl and dunk in the crumpets to fully saturate.

Heat the oil in a large frying pan, then fry the crumpets for 2 minutes on each side until golden and puffy.

Serve with spoonfuls of the blueberry compote on top, a big dollop of crème fraîche and a drizzle of maple syrup.

SWAP

Substitute the blueberries with any seasonal fruits that you like – the same method works for plums, peaches, strawberries and pears!

TIME: 15 MINUTES   **SERVES: 2**   **VEGGIE**

Coconut Caramel Overnight Oats

THE DISH

With just a little bit of prep the night before, you've got a tasty breakfast that feels like dessert. Worth it? Absolutely.

INGREDIENTS

200g **jumbo rolled oats** (check the label if making gluten-free)
2 **oranges**
1 x 400ml tin of **coconut milk**
80g **dark brown sugar**
30g **coconut flakes**
8 **figs** (approx. 270g)
salt

METHOD

In a bowl, combine the oats with the zest of a quarter of an orange, 400ml of water and a big pinch of salt. Stir, cover and pop in the fridge for at least 2 hours, or overnight.

To make the coconut caramel, add the coconut milk and half of the sugar to a saucepan. Set over a medium-high heat and bring to a boil. Reduce to a simmer, stirring occasionally, for 25–30 minutes until reduced, thickened and dark brown. Transfer to an airtight container.

Preheat the oven to 170°C fan.

Spread out the coconut flakes onto a baking tray and toast in the oven for 4–7 minutes, until golden.

Meanwhile, cut a cross in the top of each of the figs and stuff each one with the remaining sugar. Add to a baking tray and roast for 5–10 minutes until the sugar has melted and the figs are tender. Allow to cool, then pull the figs apart.

Peel and segment the oranges.

To serve, give the oats a stir to loosen, adding a splash of water if necessary. Divide between 4 bowls and top with a generous drizzle of coconut caramel, roasted figs, orange segments and toasted coconut flakes.

Miso Beans on Toast

THE DISH

Yes, this recipe is technically in the breakfast section, but you can enjoy these beans at literally any time of the day. They're deeply savoury and on just the right side of spicy. Meet your new nothing-in-the-fridge staple.

INGREDIENTS

300g **cherry tomatoes**
2 tbsp **extra virgin olive oil**, plus extra to drizzle
2 **garlic cloves**, grated
1 large **red chilli**, ½ grated, ½ sliced
2 tbsp **white miso paste**
1 x 400g tin of **butter beans**, drained and rinsed
2 slices of **sourdough**
salt and **black pepper**

METHOD

Add the tomatoes to a large, dry frying pan and cook for 6–7 minutes over a medium heat until charred and blistered on the outside. Reserve about 10 tomatoes for garnish. Add the remaining tomatoes to a blender or use a stick blender to whizz until smooth. Set aside.

Reduce the heat under the frying pan and add the olive oil. Add the garlic and the grated red chilli to the pan, frying for 2 minutes until fragrant – you may need to add a splash of water if your pan is too hot to ensure they don't burn. Add the miso paste and fry for 1 minute before adding the blitzed tomato sauce and half a tinful of water. Simmer for 10 minutes until reduced.

Add the beans and cook for 5 minutes until softened. Season to taste.

Toast the sourdough, then top with the miso beans, garnishing with a few blistered cherry tomatoes, a drizzle of olive oil and a few slices of the remaining red chilli. Finish with a grind of black pepper.

SWAP

Cannellini or haricot beans would also be lovely here.

Eggy Crumpets with Goat's Cheese + Corn

THE DISH

The kind of goat's cheese you ideally want to use here is the one that comes in a pyramid-shaped tub – it's so soft and creamy and melts gently into the eggs. You genuinely won't believe they weren't made with butter.

INGREDIENTS

1 **corn on the cob**, kernels cut off
12 **cherry tomatoes**
4 **eggs**
4 **crumpets**
2 tbsp **extra virgin olive oil**
60g soft, creamy **goat's cheese**
a few sprigs of **tarragon**, leaves picked
salt and **black pepper**

METHOD

Set a large, dry frying pan over a medium heat and, once hot, add the corn kernels and cherry tomatoes. Allow to blister and cook for 6–7 minutes until the tomatoes are wrinkly and starting to turn black, and the corn is deeply charred.

Crack the eggs into a small bowl and whisk well with a fork. Season with ¼ teaspoon of salt and a few grinds of black pepper.

Before you cook the eggs, pop the crumpets in the toaster for 3 minutes until they are golden and crisp.

Add the oil to a non-stick saucepan set over a medium-low heat, then pour in the eggs. Stir constantly with a silicone spatula, scraping up the egg from the bottom of the pan for 2–3 minutes until there are no visible bits of raw egg, but the scramble mixture is still very soft. Stir through half of the goat's cheese and turn off the heat.

Heap the cheesy scrambled eggs onto the crumpets, then scatter over the corn and tomatoes. Dollop the remaining goat's cheese on top and finish with tarragon leaves and a grind of black pepper.

6 Ways to Perfect Eggs

Nothing says 'it's going to be a good day today' like a beautiful sunny-side-up egg. Eggs are versatile, filling and easy to prepare in just a few minutes. Here's how to make the most of your morning eggs.

1. SCRAMBLED

If you're after silky scrambled eggs, add at least a tablespoon of milk (for creaminess) and a tablespoon of water (for fluffiness) to your mixture and whisk well. Make sure you season eggs *before* you scramble them – salt helps to break down the egg protein, avoiding rubbery eggs. Cooking eggs over a low heat with plenty of olive oil or butter and stirring constantly with a silicone spatula will help you attain that perfect creamy consistency. Turn off the heat as soon as you can't see any more liquid egg, to prevent overcooking. We love livening up a scramble with chopped herbs, hot sauce, fish sauce or a whack of grated cheese.

2. FRIED

There are a few different ways to fry an egg, and you should always think about the result you're trying to achieve before you decide how to cook them. If you want a crispy, lacy base and bubbly whites, you're going to want to cook them in smoking hot oil, basting the white with oil as you go. If you prefer a softer egg, coat the base of your pan in oil and cook the egg over a low heat, covering the pan with a lid to allow residual steam to cook the top. To ramp up the flavour, consider frying your eggs in things that *aren't* olive oil – a few tablespoons of pesto, harissa, 'nduja or crispy chilli oil can go a long way.

3. POACHED

Poaching an egg isn't as difficult or daunting as people make it seem. Just remember, *everyone* gets wispy bits – that's fine! Start by bringing a large pan of water to a boil, then reduce the heat to a gentle simmer and add 2 teaspoons of white wine vinegar. This will help the egg hold its shape. Crack your egg into the pan as close to the surface as you can and stir the water a few times as it cooks, to keep things from sticking. To check if your egg is done, use a slotted spoon to lift it out and give it a poke – if it feels way too soft and jiggly, it's not ready. If the white is firm and the yolk still has a bit of give, it's good to eat.

4. BOILED

For eggs that have been kept in the fridge, and are going to be plonked straight into boiling water, here are our rough cooking time guides:

Soft-boiled: 4 minutes, 30 seconds + 1 minute resting before cracking open

Jammy: 6 minutes + 1 minute resting before cracking open

Hard-boiled: 8 minutes and up!

If you're peeling your boiled eggs, it's easiest to do that in a bowl of cold water. Simply crack the shell all over and pop the egg into the cold water as you peel.

5. BAKED EGGS

You can bake your eggs in any sauce or mass of tender vegetables, really. Shakshuka is just the tip of the iceberg. Try adding aubergine, courgette, pepper and onion to a tomato sauce for a ratatouille-inspired brunch recipe. Or simply sweat down a mound of sliced leek with fresh thyme and garlic before adding cream and cracking in your eggs with a few ribbons of smoked salmon. Our main piece of advice is to avoid sticking your eggs under the grill once they're nestled in their new home or they can develop a funky, chewy skin on top – a low oven or cooked over the hob with a lid on works perfectly.

6. OMELETTES + FRITTATAS

Something to consider before making an omelette or frittata is whether you need to cook any of your ingredients before you start. No one wants raw onion in their omelette. The general consensus is that you should fry everything off in the same non-stick pan you're going to whack your eggs into later. Moderation is key, though; you don't want your omelette to be overloaded or it won't fold, and too many heavy ingredients in a frittata won't allow it to puff up. Show a little restraint and you'll thank yourself later.

Spring Onion + Kimchi Pancake

THE DISH

Inspired by a Korean kimchijeon, this is a fantastically crispy (and fantastically tasty) brunch-friendly showstopper that takes very little time to cook.

INGREDIENTS

3 **spring onions**
350g **kimchi**, roughly chopped
80g **plain flour**
1 tbsp **soy sauce**, plus extra for dipping
1 tsp **caster sugar**
1 **egg**, beaten
2 tbsp **vegetable oil**
salt and **black pepper**

METHOD

Finely slice 2 of the spring onions. Thinly shred the remaining spring onion into long strips and pop it into cold water to make it go curly.

Add the kimchi and sliced spring onions to a large mixing bowl along with the flour, soy sauce, sugar and a pinch of salt and pepper.

Add the beaten egg to the kimchi mix and give it a good stir. Set aside.

Add the oil to a large frying pan set over a medium-high heat. Once the oil is quite hot (but not smoking hot), add the kimchi mix to the pan and use the back of a spatula to flatten it down. Cook for a few minutes on each side until crispy and golden. If you struggle to flip the pancake in the pan, you can flip it onto a large plate, then slide it back into the pan.

Scatter with the curly spring onions, then dip your kimchi pancake into soy sauce before eating.

Hash Brown Butty

THE DISH

A hefty vegan one for slightly sore Sunday morning heads. Brown sauce's distinct and tangy flavour makes it an essential here – don't swap it for ketchup. Or else.

INGREDIENTS

4 **hash browns**
2 **portobello mushrooms**
2 tbsp **olive oil**
2 **vegan cheese slices**
200g **spinach**
2 **baps**
3 tbsp **brown sauce**
salt and **black pepper**

METHOD

Preheat the oven to 200°C fan.

Pop the hash browns and mushrooms (stem side up) on a baking tray, drizzle with 1 tablespoon of oil and season the mushrooms. Roast for 15–20 minutes, turning the hash browns and mushrooms halfway through the cooking time. Drain the mushrooms of any liquid at the same time. The hash browns should be deeply golden and the mushrooms should be tender and browned.

Lay a cheese slice on top of each of the cooked mushrooms and return to the oven for 1 minute until slightly melted.

In the meantime, wilt down the spinach in a frying pan over a low heat with the remaining olive oil. It helps to pop a lid on for the first minute or so to get it going. Season well with salt and pepper and squeeze out any excess liquid.

Assemble your butties by splitting each bap in half and layering on some spinach, followed by 2 hash browns, a cheesy mushroom, 1½ tablespoons of brown sauce and then the lid.

TIME: 30 MINUTES   **SERVES: 2**   **VEGAN**

Peanut Chilli Toast

THE DISH

This one is inspired by our friend What Willy Cook and his love of satay toast. He uses Bovril on his, but we're Team Marmite forever. Which, thankfully, also makes this breakfast vegan-friendly. That's what we call a win-win situation.

INGREDIENTS

1 slice of **sourdough**
2 tbsp **peanut butter**
½ tsp **yeast extract** (we like Marmite)
1 tsp **crispy chilli oil**
1 **spring onion**, finely sliced

METHOD

Toast your slice of sourdough.

Once your toast is ready, spread it with peanut butter. Then drizzle over the yeast extract and crispy chilli oil and garnish with the spring onion slices to serve.

TIME: 5 MINUTES   SERVES: 1   VEGAN   31

Hot Honey Halloumi French Toast

THE DISH

Hot honey has the world in a chokehold for good reason. Spicy and sweet, it's exactly what you want to be tossing your halloumi in. Loaded up onto a fudgy slab of French toast, this makes for an extremely louche start to the day.

INGREDIENTS

150ml **honey**
1 tsp **chilli powder**
2 tsp **olive oil**
250g **halloumi**, sliced into 8 pieces
6 **eggs**
8 slices of **sourdough**
a handful of **flat leaf parsley** leaves,
   picked in small sprigs
salt

METHOD

Add the honey and chilli powder to a small saucepan. Cook over a medium heat until the honey has liquified and turned red – this should take a couple of minutes. Set aside.

Set a frying pan over a medium-high heat, add a drizzle of olive oil and the halloumi slices. Fry for a couple of minutes on each side until deeply golden, then remove the slices and set aside and keep warm.

Beat the eggs in a wide dish with a big pinch of salt.

Heat the frying pan over a medium-high heat with a drizzle of olive oil.

Meanwhile, dunk the slices of sourdough in the egg mixture, a slice at a time, letting each piece soak for up to 20 seconds.

Shake off the excess egg mixture, then add a couple of slices at a time to the hot pan. Fry for 3 minutes on each side until golden.

Toss the halloumi slices in the honey saucepan to coat.

To serve, add 2 pieces of toast to each plate, then 2 pieces of halloumi on top. Drizzle over a little extra hot honey, then sprinkle with some parsley sprigs to serve.

TIME: 35 MINUTES   **SERVES: 4**   **VEGGIE   33**

Chorizo, Tomato + Feta Omelette

THE DISH

We've folded a triple threat of chorizo, feta and fresh oregano into a silky omelette that you won't be able to get enough of. This one has Sunday morning written all over it.

INGREDIENTS

100g **chorizo** (check the label if making gluten-free), diced in 1cm cubes
200g **cherry tomatoes**
olive oil, to fry
2 tsp **oregano** leaves, ½ finely chopped
1 tsp **smoked paprika**
6 **eggs**
60g **feta**
salt and **black pepper**

METHOD

Set a large frying pan over a medium heat and add the chorizo, cherry tomatoes, a good pinch of salt and a splash of olive oil. Cook for about 7 minutes until the chorizo is crispy and the tomatoes begin to collapse. Use a wooden spoon to help pop the tomatoes.

Add the finely chopped oregano and the smoked paprika, stir and transfer to a bowl. Set aside.

To make 1 omelette, return the frying pan to a medium heat and add a splash of olive oil. In a bowl, whisk 3 eggs with a pinch of salt and add to the pan.

Scramble the eggs for about 30 seconds to break up the curds as they cook. When the mix is about half cooked, swirl it around in the pan so the whole base is covered.

Allow to cook for another few seconds, then add half of the chorizo and tomato mixture to the centre.

Fold the omelette over, leaving some filling exposed. Transfer to a plate, crumble over half of the feta, sprinkle over some oregano leaves to garnish and finish with a grind of black pepper. Repeat to make 2 omelettes.

TIME: 25 MINUTES   **SERVES: 2**   **GLUTEN-FREE**

Parmesan Crispy Eggs + Rostis

THE DISH

Breakfast potatoes are elite, and these rostis might just be at the top of the heap. Grating Parmesan under the eggs gives you an extra layer of crisp, lacy texture. Once you try 'em like this, you won't want to eat your fried eggs any other way.

INGREDIENTS

1kg **Maris Piper potatoes**, peeled and grated
1 **onion**, grated
2 tbsp **vegetable oil**
75g **Parmesan**, finely grated, plus extra
  to garnish
4 **eggs**
a handful of **chives**, finely chopped
hot sauce (check the label if making
  gluten-free), to serve
salt and **black pepper**

METHOD

Preheat the oven to 160°C fan.

Line a colander with a clean tea towel. Tip in the grated potato and onion, then gather the top up to tighten it and squeeze out all the excess liquid you can.

Tip the dry, grated potato into a bowl. Add a pinch of salt and a generous grinding of black pepper, then mix to combine with your hands.

Pour the oil into a frying pan and set over a medium-high heat. Add small handfuls of the potato mixture a couple at a time, pushing down on them with a spatula to flatten. Fry for about 3 minutes on each side until they are super crispy and golden. Drain on kitchen paper, then transfer your rostis to the oven to keep warm while you cook the rest.

When all the rostis are cooked, move on to the eggs. In the same pan, sprinkle in enough Parmesan to lightly cover the base of the pan and crack in the eggs. Add more Parmesan over the egg whites, then fry for about 2 minutes. The base should get very golden, and the whites should bubble up nicely.

To serve, put 2 rostis on each plate and top with a fried egg. Sprinkle over some chives and the remaining Parmesan, then pour over a little hot sauce.

TIP

If you have a food processor, the grating attachment makes light work of the prep.

TIME: 30 MINUTES   SERVES: 4   **GLUTEN-FREE   37**

Rhubarb-Stuffed Croissants

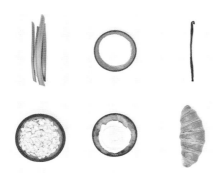

THE DISH

A pretty darn perfect brunch recipe. Crème fraîche has a lovely tang that cuts through the butteriness of the croissant and the sweetness of the jam, with the vanilla flavour in every bite. Delicious.

INGREDIENTS

400g **rhubarb**, roughly chopped
300g **caster sugar**, plus 30g for dusting (optional)
2 **vanilla pods**
80g **flaked almonds**
8 tbsp **crème fraîche**
4 **all-butter croissants**
salt

METHOD

Add the rhubarb to a medium saucepan with the 300g sugar. Stir together over a medium heat until the rhubarb starts to release its light pink juice and becomes saucy.

Split 1 of the vanilla pods and scrape out the seeds. Add the seeds and the spent pod to the saucepan with the rhubarb. Cook until the jam reaches 104°C (use a cooking thermometer for accuracy).

Pour into a sterilised jar and pop the lid on. Allow to cool. This will keep in the fridge for 1–2 weeks.

Preheat the oven to 160°C fan.

Spread out the flaked almonds on a baking tray and toast in the oven for 10–11 minutes until golden brown.

Split the second vanilla pod, scrape out the seeds and beat them into the crème fraîche with a pinch of salt, until thickened and approaching stiff peaks.

Warm the croissants in the oven for 2–3 minutes until crunchy and dark brown. Cut each croissant open widthways with a serrated knife and spread the bottom half with the rhubarb jam. Dollop on the crème fraîche and top with toasted almonds.

Sandwich on the lids and get stuck in. If you want, you can blitz 30g of sugar into a powder to dust over the croissants!

TIME: 35 MINUTES + COOLING   **SERVES: 4**   **VEGGIE**

Mortadella Pizza

THE DISH

We're obsessed with mortadella at the moment and you will be, too, after you've made this mort-heavy pizza. This recipe makes a little bit too much pistachio paste but trust us when we say that you're going to want to put it on anything within arm's reach. A slice of toast? A spoon? The sky's the limit.

INGREDIENTS

70g **shelled pistachios**
20g **Parmesan**
½ **lemon**, juiced
5 tbsp **extra virgin olive oil**
1 **plain pizza base**
100g **mozzarella**
6 slices of **mortadella**
salt and **black pepper**

METHOD

Preheat the oven to 180°C fan.

Place the pistachios on a baking tray and toast in the oven for around 6 minutes.

Once toasted, blitz 50g of pistachios in a food processor with 15g of Parmesan, the lemon juice, olive oil, a pinch of salt and 3–5 tablespoons of water until a loose paste is formed.

Place the pizza base on a baking tray, then tear the mozzarella into pieces and dot over the surface. Bake for 10–12 minutes until the cheese has melted and is beginning to brown.

Roughly chop the remaining pistachios.

To serve, lay the mortadella slices over the pizza, dollop over the pistachio paste, sprinkle with the chopped pistachios and the remaining Parmesan. Finish with a good grind of black pepper.

SWAP

You could also use a pre-made focaccia for the base.

TIME: 25 MINUTES   SERVES: 2

Gochujang Kimcheese Toastie

THE DISH

Kimchi and cheese are soul mates. There are no two ways about it. Those star-crossed lovers come together in perfect harmony in this hefty toastie.

INGREDIENTS

2 tbsp **gochujang paste**
4 tbsp **mayonnaise**
4 slices of **sourdough**
8 slices of **pre-sliced Cheddar cheese**
2 **spring onions**, thinly sliced
60g **kimchi**

METHOD

In a small bowl, mix together the gochujang and 2 tablespoons of the mayonnaise. Spread 1 side of each of the 4 slices of sourdough with the mixture.

Turn the bread over, and spread the remaining mayo on the other side of the 4 slices of bread.

Take 2 slices of the sourdough and lay 4 slices of Cheddar on each piece, on top of the gochujang mixture. Sprinkle the spring onions on top of the Cheddar and top with the kimchi. Sandwich on the remaining 2 slices of bread (with the gochujang mixture facing inwards).

Place in a cold frying pan, then set over a hob and turn on the heat to medium-low. Cook for 2–3 minutes on each side, pressing down regularly with a spatula until the bread is toasted and the cheese has melted. Slice up and serve.

Sausage + Taleggio Ciabatta

THE DISH

The colossal hangover sammie of your dreams. Squishing the sausages and making giant patties means that they cook faster and you get a nice even layer of sausage throughout the sandwich. You can find guindilla chilli peppers in most good supermarkets but feel free to sub them out for those kebab-style pickled chillies you can get from the corner shop.

INGREDIENTS

6 **sausages**, meat squeezed out
1 **ciabatta**
10 **guindilla chilli peppers**, roughly chopped
4 tbsp **extra virgin olive oil**
3 **garlic cloves**, grated
200g **spring greens** or **cavolo nero**,
   thickly shredded
150g **Taleggio**, sliced
black pepper

METHOD

Put the sausage meat into a bowl and knead briefly with your hands to create a homogenous mix, then split in half. Shape into 2 long and flat patties – each roughly the same size and shape as half of the ciabatta. It can help to do this between 2 pieces of baking paper.

Split the ciabatta and toast in a dry pan set over a high heat. Once toasted, set aside and reserve the pan.

Put the chillies and the olive oil into a bowl and blitz with a stick blender until you have a rough paste. Alternatively, you can chop the chillies very finely and mix them by hand.

Set the reserved pan over a medium heat and add the garlic and spring greens with a splash of water. Sauté until wilted. Remove from the pan, squeeze out any excess liquid and set aside, returning the pan to the heat.

Peeling off the top slice of baking paper from the sausage (if you used it), flip each patty directly onto the pan and peel back the remaining baking paper. Fry for 2 minutes on each side until golden and caramelised. When you've cooked one side of each patty and flipped them over, add the Taleggio slices on top and let the cheese melt.

Layer up the sandwich with the chilli paste spread on the bottom slice of ciabatta, followed by some wilted spring greens, a cheesy sausage patty on each side and a grind of black pepper. Finally, top with the remaining ciabatta lid, cut in half and serve.

    TIME: 30 MINUTES   **SERVES: 2**

Lamb Neck + Mint Flatbreads

THE DISH

This bolshy flavour combination was inspired by Helen Graves, who is a total master of all things grilled. Jarred artichokes have a delicate sharpness to them and are delicious when partnered up with a fiery garlic yoghurt and tender yoghurt-marinated meat. Don't skimp on the mint – it gives everything a lovely burst of freshness.

INGREDIENTS

1 **lamb neck** portion (approx. 400g)
125g thick **Greek yoghurt** (we like Total Fage 5%)
a small handful of **mint** leaves, plus extra to serve
1 **garlic clove**, finely grated
3 **flatbreads**
150g **jarred artichokes** (drained weight)
salt and **black pepper**

METHOD

Pop the lamb neck in a small bowl and add 2 tablespoons of the yoghurt. Season generously with salt, toss well to coat and set aside to marinate for at least 30 minutes and up to 2 hours.

Meanwhile, finely chop the mint and add to a bowl with the garlic and remaining yoghurt.

When the lamb has finished marinating, preheat a griddle pan over a high heat. Wipe any excess yoghurt marinade off the lamb and grill for 3 minutes on each side – take care as the lamb fat can spit. Transfer the lamb to a plate and set aside to rest for 10 minutes.

Add the flatbreads to the same pan to toast on each side and absorb the lamb juices.

To serve, thinly slice the lamb. Add a dollop of the garlic–mint yoghurt to a flatbread, followed by a few lamb slices, artichokes, a grind of black pepper and extra mint leaves.

Red Curry
Prawn Burgers

THE DISH

Don't be put off if you're not a huge spicy food fan, the curry paste injects a lovely aroma and flavour without knocking your socks off. If you do want it hot, though, you have our explicit permission to go wild and whack in a load of red chillies.

INGREDIENTS

200g **raw king prawns**
1 tbsp **Thai red curry paste**
30g **coriander**, stalks and leaves separated
75g **mayonnaise**
2 **burger buns**
3 tbsp **vegetable oil**
¼ **cucumber**, peeled into ribbons
salt and **black pepper**

METHOD

Add the prawns, curry paste and coriander stalks to a food processor and pulse until combined. Alternatively, you can finely chop everything and mix well by hand (it helps if you have wet hands so it doesn't stick to you!). Form into 2 burger patties and chill in the fridge for 30 minutes until firmed up.

Meanwhile, blitz most of the coriander leaves with the mayonnaise until you have a vibrant green sauce. Season well.

Set a large frying pan over a medium heat, split the buns in half and toast cut-side down until golden. Set aside.

Add the oil to the same pan and fry the patties for 2–4 minutes on each side until they're a nice golden colour and cooked through.

Spread some coriander mayo onto the base of each toasted bun, then top with a prawn patty, cucumber ribbons and the remaining coriander leaves. Add a little mayo to the burger lids, then sandwich a lid on each one.

TIME: 20 MINUTES + CHILLING   SERVES: 2

Tart-iflette

THE DISH

We love tartiflette. We love pastry. So, we decided to turn a tartiflette into an actual tart. Clever, huh? Creamy potatoes and pancetta go beautifully with the crisp puff pastry. If you can't get your hands on Reblochon, Camembert will do the trick.

INGREDIENTS

150g **pancetta lardons**
2 **onions**, finely sliced
1 sheet of **ready-rolled puff pastry**
500g small **waxy potatoes**, peeled and sliced
    into ½cm pieces
300ml **double cream**
225g **Reblochon**, sliced
salt and **black pepper**

METHOD

Preheat the oven to 210°C fan.

Set a frying pan over a medium heat. Add the pancetta and fry gently until the fat has rendered out and the pieces are crisp. Remove the pancetta from the pan with a slotted spoon, reserving the fat.

Add the onions to the pancetta fat and fry for 20 minutes until caramelised.

Meanwhile, unroll the puff pastry sheet and place it on a baking tray lined with baking paper. Using a sharp knife, score a 2cm border around the pastry, taking care not to pierce all the way through. Pop it in the oven for 12 minutes until golden and risen.

Once the onions are golden and soft, add the potatoes to the pan. Fry for 5 minutes, then pour in the double cream and 150ml of water. Season with salt and pepper, then gently simmer for 15 minutes until the potatoes have just softened.

Add half of the Reblochon slices to the potato pan. Allow it to gently melt. Check the seasoning of the potato mixture, adding more salt and pepper if needed.

Spoon the mixture into the centre of the pastry, avoiding the border and spreading out with the back of a spoon so it is evenly distributed. Top with the reserved pancetta lardons and remaining Reblochon, then bake for another 7 minutes in the oven. The Reblochon should go all melty and gooey on the top.

Allow the tart to rest for 5 minutes, then top with a grind of black pepper, cut into pieces and serve.

TIME: 1 HOUR   SERVES: 4

Smoky Tomato + Aubergine Sandwich

THE DISH

Sweet, nutty, pickled, smoky and peppery – this has all the elements required to make the perfect sandwich. A proper two-hander, this.

INGREDIENTS

400g **Datterini tomatoes**
155ml **olive oil**, plus extra to drizzle
3 **aubergines**, sliced into 1cm-thick rounds
100g **smoked almonds**
1 x 200g jar of **guindilla chilli peppers** (3–4 chillies per sandwich), plus brining liquid
4 chunks of **focaccia**
90g **rocket**
salt and **black pepper**

METHOD

Add half of the tomatoes to a small saucepan with 60ml of olive oil. Set over a medium heat and simmer for 30 minutes until the tomatoes have softened. Season with plenty of freshly cracked pepper and set aside to cool.

Meanwhile, add the slices of aubergine to a large bowl and season generously with salt, tossing well to make sure they are evenly coated. Transfer to a sieve and set over the bowl for 20 minutes until beads of moisture appear on the surface of the aubergine.

Add 45ml of the olive oil to a medium bowl. Halve the rest of the tomatoes and stir them through the olive oil. Season with salt and allow to macerate until needed.

Wash any excess salt off the aubergines and dry thoroughly with kitchen paper. Place a saucepan over a medium heat and add the remaining 50ml of olive oil. Once the oil is hot, cook the aubergines until they have softened and are golden on both sides, 7–10 minutes. You may have to do this in batches.

Once the confit tomatoes have cooled, add them with their oil and the smoked almonds to a food processor. Blitz until a paste forms. Season with some of the guindilla chilli brine.

Halve and toast the focaccia. Spread the confit tomato and smoked almond pesto over the bottom slices of focaccia, then top each slice with the aubergines, macerated tomatoes, chillies and rocket. Drizzle over some olive oil and top with some more confit tomato and smoked almond pesto before squishing on the focaccia lids. Finish with a grind of black pepper.

TIME: 45 MINUTES **SERVES: 4** **VEGAN** 55

6 Steps to a
Perfect Sandwich

So, you've got a 6-ingredient limit and you want to build the perfect sandwich? Easy. Here's what you should consider to create the perfect sarnie. We've even thrown in a few helpful sandwich architecture tips for good measure.

1. APPROPRIATE VIBE

First off, think about where you want to enjoy your sandwich. If it's a 'lunch box at work' vibe, you're going to want to avoid toasted bread, overly soggy fillings or heat-sensitive elements. If it's a 'stuff-it-in-your-backpack' jobby for after a long hike, you're going to want to make that bad boy much bigger than you thought – you'll be ravenous by the time you end up eating. If it's a sandwich designed to be eaten on a plate at home, you can go to town with warm, melty elements, so capitalise on that luxury.

2. BREAD CHOICES

The sandwich is your oyster when it comes to bread choices. Our absolute favourite is a focaccia – it has plenty of pockets to hold in your sauce, a perfect balance between soft spongy insides and a slight oily crunch on the outside. We'd recommend a baguette when your fillings are on the smaller size and can benefit from the structural integrity and bite of a shattering crust. There's a time and a place for pappy white bread when it comes to traditional butties or bacon sarnies, but always try and go for the thickest you can find, or it'll squish down too much and feel a bit school trippy. Try to think outside of the box with your choices. Could you go for a bread that already has added flavour like a seeded loaf or an olive ciabatta? Go wild.

3. SUFFICIENT CRUNCH

Crunch can come from a whole host of things in your sammie of choice. Is it a breadcrumbed fish finger or chicken escalope? Could it be a load of iceberg lettuce for an unparalleled fresh and juicy crunch? Pickles for a bit of funk and acidity? Crisp fruit and vegetables like cucumber, apple or carrot? Crunchy add-ons like crisps, Bombay Mix or crispy onions? Maybe your crunch is coming from the bread itself via a crusty roll or a toasted multigrain slice. Whatever sandwich you're making, try to make sure you're aiming for at least one crunchy element to ensure the optimum eating experience.

4. SAUCINESS

There's nothing worse than a dry sanger, is there? Don't be stingy with your mayo/butter/mustard/spread of choice and consider layering up multiple saucy elements at the same time. Don't be afraid to dress the leaves of your salad, and remember that melted cheese and soft cheese like burrata can also bring some much needed juiciness to the party. There is a line here to toe, though. You have to think about the speed at which you're going to eat your sandwich because, if you do make it a bit on the wetter side, you'll need to snaffle it quickly before it leaks out all over your hands and drips down your forearms. We don't need to tell you that's not a good look.

5. UP THE FLAVOUR

One of the cold, hard realities of making a sandwich is that putting anything delicious in between two pieces of stodgy carbohydrate means you're inevitably going to dilute the flavour of the filling. To combat this, make sure you're adequately seasoning the insides and hitting each layer of your construction with a sprinkle of salt. Try to think of some extra flavour bombs you can add to your sauces as well – lemon juice, vinegar, chilli sauce, capers, herbs or even a bit of MSG can really help make everything sing.

6. ARCHITECTURE

The order in which you layer up the elements of your sandwich is vitally important. Sauce on both sides so everything sticks together is essential. Always keep your sturdiest fillings on the outside and the softest/soggiest closest to the middle. Think about how you cut your bread, too – if you're using a baguette or ciabatta it's worth thinking about keeping one seam attached when you slice it horizontally to prevent all your lovely ingredients from falling out. Sometimes, if you've got a particularly loaded sandwich, it can help to tightly wrap it up in baking paper or foil before cutting. Wrapping it up like that will also help when it comes to transporting your sanger from A to B.

All the Onions Smashburger

THE DISH

If you hadn't already guessed from the name of this recipe, onions are the star of the show here. We've got them three ways – a caramelised onion mayo, crispy fried slivers of onion and in their natural naked state. Needless to say, they work wonders with beef patties and bright orange melted cheese. This tastes like the kind of thing you'd get in an NYC bodega, and we are here for it.

INGREDIENTS

6 tbsp **olive oil**
3 large **onions**, finely sliced
800g **beef mince (12% fat)**
8 **pre-packaged cheese slices**
100g **mayonnaise**
4 **burger buns**
¼ **iceberg lettuce**, shredded
salt

METHOD

Heat 5 tablespoons of olive oil in a frying pan over a medium-low heat and add 2 of the onions, then cook for about 30 minutes. Add a splash of water occasionally and stir frequently to stop them burning. They will soften, then start to stick slightly and caramelise.

Set a small frying pan over a medium-high heat with a generous glug of olive oil. Add half of the remaining onion and fry for about 5 minutes until golden. This may happen at different rates for different onion strands – lift each out as they turn golden and place on a plate lined with kitchen paper.

Season the mince with salt, mixing loosely with your hands without compressing it too much. Divide the meat into 8 equal-sized pieces and roll each into a rough ball. Flatten each ball with the base of a heavy pan.

Set a frying pan over a very high heat. Fry each patty for 2 minutes until deeply caramelised. The burgers should be very flat and crisp. They may need to be fried in batches depending on the size of your pan.

Add a slice of cheese to each burger once they have been flipped, plus a splash of water on top, then add a lid to the pan. Cook for 2 minutes until the cheese has melted and the base is caramelised. Once the caramelised onions are cool, mix them with the mayonnaise.

Preheat the grill to medium-high. Split the buns and toast them under the grill. Once toasted, spread caramelised onion mayo on the base of each bun. Add lettuce and 2 patties, then sprinkle over the raw sliced onion and the crispy onions. Spread more onion mayo on the lid of each bun and sandwich on top.

TIME: 1 HOUR   SERVES: 4

Bombay Fish Finger Sandwich

THE DISH

Whizzing up Bombay Mix to make the crust for these fish fingers takes your favourite childhood dinner to the next level. Baking the fish fingers helps them retain their shape while still keeping them nice and crisp to contrast with the squishy white bread and tangy curry mayo. Oh, and let's not forget the obligatory shredded iceberg. Nostalgia's never tasted this good.

INGREDIENTS

200g **Bombay Mix**
5 tbsp **tikka curry paste**
150g **mayonnaise**
4 skinless and boneless **cod fillets** (approx. 500g), sliced into 3cm-wide strips
8 thick slices of **white bread**
¼ **iceberg lettuce**, shredded
salt and **black pepper**

METHOD

Preheat the oven to 200°C fan.

Add the Bombay Mix to a food processor and blitz to coarse crumbs. Pour these into a shallow bowl.

Add 3 tablespoons of curry paste to another shallow bowl with 40g of mayonnaise and loosen with 30ml of water. Whisk until smooth and season well.

Dip the cod strips into the curry paste mix one at a time so that they are totally covered, then shake off the excess. Dip them in the Bombay Mix and toss so they are coated.

Pop a sheet of baking paper on a baking tray. Evenly space the fish fingers on the tray, then put in the oven to cook for 12–15 minutes until the crumbs are lightly golden and the fish is cooked through.

Mix the remaining 2 tablespoons of tikka curry paste with the remaining 110g of mayonnaise in a bowl.

Spread each bread slice with mayonnaise, then lay the fish fingers on 4 slices. Top with lettuce, then sandwich each one closed with the remaining bread slices. Serve with a grinding of black pepper, if you like.

TIME: 35 MINUTES   **SERVES: 4**

Beetroot, Carrot + Hummus Tart

THE DISH

This is an easy make-ahead recipe that tastes just as good at room temperature, making it perfect for a picnic or al fresco vibes. Use the creamiest hummus you can find – it really does make all the difference.

INGREDIENTS

1 sheet of **vegan ready-rolled puff pastry**
1 **beetroot** (approx. 150g), peeled and grated
2 **carrots** (approx. 100g), peeled and grated
a large handful of **coriander**, stalks and leaves separated
1½ tbsp **nigella seeds**
2 tbsp **extra virgin olive oil**, plus extra to drizzle
200g **hummus**
salt and **black pepper**

METHOD

Preheat the oven to 180°C fan.

Roll out the puff pastry sheet and transfer it to a baking tray, keeping it on the baking paper it comes on. Score an inner rectangular border 1½cm around the edge with a sharp knife, taking care not to cut all the way through the pastry.

Bake for 12–14 minutes until deeply golden and puffy. Use a spoon to press down the inner rectangle, so the border is raised.

Add the beetroot and carrots to a bowl. Very finely chop the coriander stalks and half of the leaves and add to the bowl, along with the nigella seeds and olive oil. Mix well to combine, then season generously.

When the pastry is cooked, spread the hummus on the base and top with the grated root vegetable mixture. Garnish with the remaining coriander leaves and finish with an extra drizzle of olive oil.

TIME: 20 MINUTES   SERVES: 4   VEGAN   63

Farinata with Fig + Olive Salsa

THE DISH

Crispy, custardy farinata topped with a sweet and salty salsa – super quick, very easy and extremely delicious. What's not to love?

INGREDIENTS

110g **chickpea (gram) flour**
10g **rosemary** leaves, roughly chopped
190ml **water**
8 tbsp **olive oil**, plus extra to drizzle
1 x 160g jar of **pitted Kalamata olives**, drained
6 **figs**, chopped into 1cm chunks
25g **flat leaf parsley**, roughly chopped
1 **lemon**, zested and juiced
salt and **black pepper**

METHOD

Add the flour, rosemary and half the water to a bowl and whisk until smooth. Then add ½ teaspoon of salt, 2 tablespoons of olive oil and the remaining water, whisking until the batter is lump-free and completely smooth. Set aside to rest for 15 minutes.

Meanwhile, lightly crush and chop the drained olives. Add the olives, figs, parsley (reserving some for garnish) and lemon zest to a bowl. Stir through the lemon juice, 2 tablespoons of olive oil and season with salt and lots of freshly cracked black pepper. Cover and set aside to marinate.

Preheat the grill to high. When the batter has rested for a full 15 minutes, set a large, ovenproof frying pan over a medium-high heat and pour in 4 tablespoons of olive oil. Once the oil is hot, pour in the batter and don't move the pan. Reduce the heat to medium and cook for 4–5 minutes, to set the bottom of the farinata – it should be crispy and visibly browning at the sides.

Place the frying pan under the grill and cook the top of the farinata until set, 3–6 minutes. Keep an eye on it so it doesn't burn.

Flip the farinata so the crispy bottom is on the top. Serve with the fig and black olive salsa, a drizzle of olive oil and the reserved parsley leaves as a garnish, plus a sprinkling of salt, if you like.

TIME: 25 MINUTES + RESTING   **SERVES: 4**   **VEGAN, GLUTEN-FREE**

Pickle Buttermilk Chicken Burgers

THE DISH

The best kind of pickles for this are those American deli-style pre-sliced pickles. Look out for stacker pickles or sliced sandwich pickles. Failing that, just buy your pickles whole and slice them yourself. Seriously – don't scrimp on the pickles, they add a sharp and briny freshness to the burger.

INGREDIENTS

6 skinless and boneless **chicken thighs**
600ml **buttermilk**
12 **pickle slices**, plus 100ml pickling liquid
3 tbsp **hot sauce** (we like Frank's, Kold or Cholula)
vegetable oil, to fry
500g **plain flour**
6 **burger buns**
salt and **black pepper**

METHOD

Pop the chicken thighs in a bowl, plastic container or sandwich bag with 400ml of buttermilk and the pickling liquid. Toss well to coat, then set aside to marinate for at least 1 hour, or up to 24 hours. If marinating for more than an hour, cover and leave in the fridge.

When you're ready to start cooking, mix the remaining 200ml of buttermilk with the hot sauce and season to taste – you want it to be sharp, hot and tangy. Set aside until ready to serve.

Pour the oil into a large saucepan or Dutch oven and fill no more than halfway up the sides. Set over a high heat. If you have one, use a cooking thermometer to check when the oil gets to 180°C.

Add the flour to a deep bowl and season very generously – you will need at least a tablespoon each of black pepper and salt to properly season the flour.

Lift a chicken thigh out of the marinade and drop it straight into the flour. Use your hands to coat it all over. Chuck it back in the marinade to make it wet again, then back into the flour to fully coat one more time – this is what gives you the crisp and craggy 'cornflake' style batter. Pop on a baking tray and repeat with the remaining chicken thighs.

Preheat the grill to its highest setting.

To test if your oil is hot enough, throw in a
little piece of the buttermilk/flour nuggets
that will be remaining in the bowl. If it sizzles,
it's ready. Fry the chicken thighs in 2 batches,
cooking for 4–6 minutes until deeply golden
and cooked through.

While the chicken is frying, lay the burger
buns, cut-side up, on a large baking tray
and grill for 1–2 minutes until lightly
toasted. When the first batch of chicken is
done, pop it on another tray on the bottom
shelf of the oven to keep warm while you fry
the second batch.

Spread the buttermilk hot sauce on a toasted
bun base, top with a chicken thigh, at least
2 pickle slices and lots more buttermilk hot
sauce. Add a grind of black pepper and top
with a toasted bun lid to sandwich.

Cheesy Onion Quiche

THE DISH

We've basically taken the flavours of a French onion soup and crammed them into a tart. The set of this is slightly less solid than a quiche, keeping a soft custardy-ness that we're extremely into.

INGREDIENTS

1 x 500g block of **shortcrust pastry**
1 tbsp **olive oil**
3 large **onions**, thinly sliced
4 sprigs of **thyme**, leaves picked, plus extra sprigs to garnish
2 **eggs**, plus 3 **yolks**
200ml **double cream**
130g **Gruyère**, grated, plus extra to serve
salt and **black pepper**

METHOD

Preheat the oven to 180°C fan.

Line a work surface with baking paper and roll out the pastry to a 2mm thickness, ensuring it is even all over.

Lift the pastry with a rolling pin and drape it carefully into a 20cm tart tin. Fold all the edges into the centre, then gradually work your way round, pushing the edges back out so you get the pastry right to the bottom corners. Trim most of the excess pastry, then leave the tin in the fridge to chill.

Set a large frying pan over a medium heat and add a generous glug of olive oil, then tip in the onions. Add the thyme leaves to the pan. Cook gently for 30–40 minutes until the onions are softened and deeply caramelised – they should be a rusty-brown colour and significantly reduced in volume. Occasionally add a splash of water to deglaze the pan if needed. Allow to cool to room temperature.

Once the tart case is firm, remove from the fridge and prick the base with a fork. Scrunch up a sheet of baking paper, then smooth it out and use it to line the tart. Pour in some baking beans or uncooked rice. Bake for 15 minutes, then remove the baking beans and baking paper and cook for a further 5–10 minutes until the base of the pastry is sandy to the touch with no visible translucent or wet patches.

METHOD CONTINUED

Reduce the oven temperature to 170°C fan.

Crack the eggs into the bowl containing the yolks, then pour in the double cream. Beat until combined.

Add the Gruyère and tip in the onions, then season with salt and lots of black pepper. Carefully pour the mixture into the pastry case, then bake for 30–40 minutes.

Allow to cool for 15 minutes before serving. Use a small, serrated knife to neaten up the pastry edges.

Finish with an extra grating of Gruyère and thyme sprigs to garnish.

TIP

You can save the egg whites you don't use for another recipe.

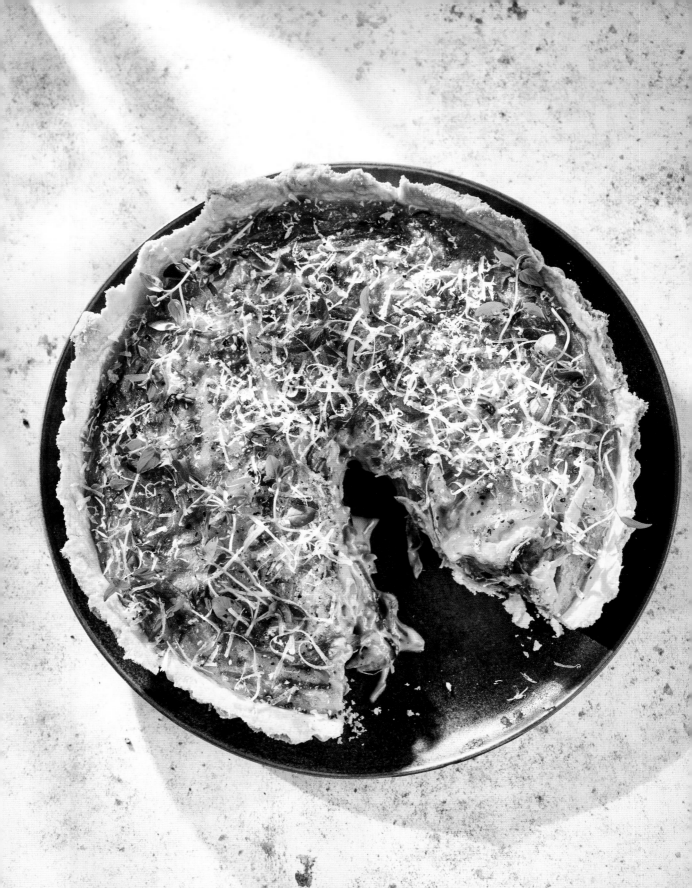

Sprout, Sausage + Stilton Focaccia

THE DISH

Prepare to make this part of your regular festive menu rotation. Shredding a sprout will convert even the most determined sprout hater into a devoted sprout stan. To up the Christmas vibes even more, try swapping the balsamic glaze for dollops of cranberry sauce.

INGREDIENTS

1 **focaccia** (approx. 350–400g)
100g **ricotta**
150g **Brussels sprouts**, shredded
2 **sausages**, meat squeezed out
75g **Stilton cheese**
2 tbsp **balsamic glaze**

METHOD

Preheat the grill to its highest setting.

Halve the focaccia widthways so it opens out like a book and the surface area is doubled – pop it on a baking tray.

Spread the ricotta over the focaccia base, right to the edges.

Scatter the Brussels sprouts over in an even layer and crumble the sausage meat over the Brussels sprouts.

Place under the grill for 12–15 minutes until the sausage is cooked through and beginning to caramelise. Watch it carefully, as most grills run at different temperatures, and you don't want it to burn.

Crumble over the Stilton in an even layer, nestling it into the gaps between the sausage and Brussels sprouts, then return to the grill for 2 minutes until the cheese has melted.

Drizzle over the balsamic glaze, then slice and serve.

TIME: 20 MINUTES   **SERVES: 4**   73

GHTER LIGHTER LI
R LIGHTER LIGHTE
GHTER LIGHTER LI
R LIGHTER LIGHTE
GHTER LIGHTER LI
R LIGHTER LIGHTE

Nectarine Sumac Salad

THE DISH

It doesn't get fresher than this. If you can't get ripe nectarines, sub them with peaches, plums, tomatoes or persimmons, depending on the season. It might look like a hell of a lot of mint but it's being used like a fragrant salad leaf here, so don't short-change yourself.

INGREDIENTS

2 ripe **nectarines**, de-stoned and cut into wedges
2 mild **green chillies**
2 **spring onions**, finely sliced
2 tbsp **sumac**
2 tbsp **extra virgin olive oil**
20g **mint** leaves
60g **feta**
salt and **black pepper**

METHOD

Put the nectarine wedges into a medium-sized bowl. Grate 1 of the green chillies on top using a microplane.

Add the spring onions, sumac, olive oil and mint leaves to the nectarines and crumble in the feta. Season generously with salt and pepper.

Toss well to coat everything. Finely slice the remaining green chilli and use to garnish.

Plate up and dig in!

TIME: 5 MINUTES   SERVES: 2   VEGGIE, GLUTEN-FREE   77

Bean, Blue Cheese + Cranberry Salad

METHOD

Bring a large pan of salted water to a boil over a medium heat and cook the green beans for 3 minutes, then drain and refresh under cold running water.

Set a frying pan over a medium heat and add the walnuts. Toast for 3–4 minutes until golden and fragrant. Finely chop a handful of the nuts and leave the rest whole.

Add the finely chopped nuts to a small bowl with the mustard, red wine vinegar and oil and whisk well to combine. Season to taste.

Assemble the salad by tossing together the beans, remaining whole walnuts and the cranberries and crumble the blue cheese over everything.

Pour over the dressing and dig in.

THE DISH

The finely chopped walnuts in the dressing add a lovely earthy, toasty note to the whole shebang.

INGREDIENTS

250g **green beans**, trimmed
80g **walnuts**
1 tbsp **Dijon mustard**
2 tbsp **red wine vinegar**
4 tbsp **extra virgin olive oil**
100g **dried cranberries**
100g **blue cheese**
salt and **black pepper**

TIME: 15 MINUTES   SERVES: 3–4 AS A SIDE   VEGGIE, GLUTEN-FREE   83

6 Go-To Salad Dressings

There aren't a huge number of overly complicated dressings in the pages that follow because (a) not everyone has the time to faff about with macerated shallots, and (b) we couldn't exactly use up all of our 6 ingredients on a single dressing, now could we? These dressings might have more ingredients than the others you'll find in this book but they're no less simple to make and will all keep for at least a week in the fridge. Guaranteed to spruce up any salad.

1. PICKLED SHALLOT DRESSING

This is a standard dressing with a bit more flare. Letting the shallots pickle before making it adds an unparalleled funk.

2 **shallots**, finely chopped
60ml **red wine vinegar**
1 tbsp **Dijon mustard**
100ml **extra virgin olive oil**
a small handful of **tarragon** leaves, finely chopped

Allow the shallots to macerate in the red wine vinegar for at least 5 minutes and for up to a maximum of 2 hours. After an adequate amount of time has elapsed, whisk in the mustard, olive oil and tarragon.

2. YOGHURT CAESAR DRESSING

A Caesar-ish dressing with all the right flavours and without the mayo.

5 tbsp **Greek yoghurt**
1 **lemon**, zested and juiced
2 tbsp **extra virgin olive oil**
2 **anchovies**, finely chopped
2 tbsp finely grated **Parmesan**
2 tbsp **capers**, finely chopped
salt and **black pepper**

Mix everything together and season to taste.

3. HARISSA LIME DRESSING

We love this drizzled over couscous and other grain-forward salads.

1 tbsp **harissa paste**
1 tbsp **tahini**
4 tbsp **extra virgin olive oil**
2 **limes**, zested and juiced
salt and **black pepper**

Mix everything together, loosening with water if needed, and season to taste.

4. MISO VINAIGRETTE

Perfect on warm veggies or a crunchy side salad.

> 2 tbsp **white miso paste**
> 1 tbsp **honey**
> 2 tbsp **sesame oil**
> 2 tbsp **vegetable oil**
> 3 tbsp **rice wine vinegar**
> 1 tbsp **soy sauce**

Whisk together until combined.

5. GARLIC & HERB DRESSING

This tastes just like a certain pizza chain's addictive dipping sauce, and you'll be bloody glad for it.

> 1 bulb of **garlic**, roasted
> a small handful of **parsley**, finely chopped
> a small handful of **chives**, finely chopped
> 2 tbsp **red wine vinegar**
> 2 tbsp **crème fraîche**
> 2 tbsp **olive oil**

Squeeze the roasted garlic from the bulb and mix it up with everything else. Simple.

6. CHIPOTLE ORANGE DRESSING

Add some excitement to your tacos or fajita bowls with this zippy dressing. It also tastes grand over charred corn.

> 1 tbsp **chipotle paste**
> 1 **orange**, zested and juiced
> 2 tbsp **white wine vinegar**
> a pinch of **dried oregano**
> 5 tbsp **extra virgin olive oil**

Mix it up, adding more chipotle paste if you like it spicy.

Larb-Style Ceviche

THE DISH

At its most basic level, ceviche is fresh raw fish that's been marinated in citrus. We've given it a Laotian-inspired twist by adding fish sauce, lime and fresh coriander. Served with crispy tortilla chips, this fresh and zesty situation is the perfect dinner party starter.

INGREDIENTS

½ small **red onion**, thinly sliced
250g skinless and boneless **pollock**, diced into 1cm pieces
½ tsp **salt**
150ml freshly squeezed **lime juice**
2 tbsp **fish sauce** (check the label if making gluten-free)
2 tbsp **caster sugar**
a small handful of **coriander** leaves, picked in small sprigs

METHOD

Place the red onion in a small bowl, cover with ice-cold water and soak for 5 minutes, then drain.

Add the pollock to a medium bowl. Season with the salt, toss gently to combine and leave for 2 minutes. This will help the fish to firm up a little so it doesn't break down when stirring in the rest of the ingredients.

Meanwhile, drain the red onion and add it to a bowl with the lime juice, fish sauce and sugar. Pour this over the fish and toss gently to combine. Cover and leave to marinate in the fridge. After 30 minutes, strain off the marinade, reserving some of the liquid.

Plate up the ceviche with a drizzle of the marinade, then top with coriander and serve with the squeezed lime wedges.

Cajun Salmon with Mango Salsa

THE DISH

A simple, quick light meal. Feel free to bulk it out with grains or rice, but it's gorgeous as is. To make it even quicker, buy pre-cut mango and give it an extra chop. Easy.

INGREDIENTS

2 tbsp **olive oil**

1½ tbsp **Cajun seasoning** (check the label if making gluten-free)

2 **salmon fillets**

1 **mango**, peeled and finely diced

½ **red onion**, finely diced

a large handful of **coriander** leaves, finely chopped

1 **lime**, zested and juiced, plus extra wedges to serve (optional)

salt and **black pepper**

METHOD

Preheat the oven to 180°C fan.

In a small bowl, mix together the oil and Cajun seasoning.

Line a baking tray with foil. Rub the Cajun oil over the salmon fillets, sprinkle with salt and pepper and bake for 8–10 minutes until the flesh is coral-coloured inside and starting to flake away.

In a small bowl, mix together the mango, red onion and coriander with the lime zest and juice.

Serve the salmon alongside the mango salsa with extra lime wedges, if you like.

SWAP

If you can't find Cajun seasoning, this is also lovely with a bit of smoked paprika.

Tomato +
Triple Shallot Salad

THE DISH

This isn't your typical tomato salad. We've freshened this sal up with funky fish sauce, lots of lime and no less than three different types of shallot – jammy ones roasted with fish sauce, quick-pickled ones scrunched up with lime and crispy fried ones for that much-needed bit of crunch. A beautiful light lunch or side dish.

INGREDIENTS

6 **banana shallots**, 4 peeled and quartered lengthways, 1 finely chopped, 1 sliced into thin rounds
4 tbsp **fish sauce** (check the label if making gluten-free)
1 tbsp **olive oil**
1 **red chilli**, finely chopped
1 **lime**, juiced, plus extra wedges to serve
vegetable oil, to fry
600g **tomatoes**, cut into irregular chunks
a handful of **mint** leaves
salt

METHOD

Add the 4 quartered shallots to a frying pan and pour over 2 tablespoons of the fish sauce, 2 tablespoons of water, the olive oil and a pinch of salt. Fry over a medium-low heat for 20–25 minutes, cut-side down, regularly adding a splash more water if the pan looks too dry. They're done when they are soft, tender and caramelised.

Meanwhile, add the finely chopped shallot and chilli to a bowl with half of the lime juice, along with a pinch of salt. Scrunch up with your hands to lightly pickle the shallot.

Pour a good glug of vegetable oil into a frying pan to coat the bottom of the pan, then add the shallot rounds. Turn on the heat to allow the oil to gently come up to temperature – this will prevent them from burning – and fry for about 5 minutes until they are golden and crisp up.

Remove the shallots from the pan with a slotted spoon, transferring them to a plate lined with kitchen paper. Leave to cool slightly.

Salt the tomatoes and leave in a bowl for 10 minutes, then toss with the remaining lime juice and the remaining 2 tablespoons of fish sauce.

Arrange the tomatoes on a platter along with the caramelised shallots. Top with the pickled shallot and chilli mixture, the crispy shallots and some fresh mint leaves. Serve with extra lime wedges, if you like.

TIME: 35 MINUTES   SERVES: 4   GLUTEN-FREE

Green Chopped Salad

THE DISH

The freshness of this salad is unparalleled. Yes, there's a lot of lime juice going on, but you really need the acid to liven this up. It keeps really well in the fridge, too, so it's a perfect packed lunch for making everyone at the office really, really jealous.

INGREDIENTS

2 **avocados**
3 **limes**, juiced
1 **green chilli**, thinly sliced
4 tbsp **extra virgin olive oil**, plus extra
   to drizzle
½ **cucumber**, sliced into irregular chunks
200g **sugar snap peas**, halved or sliced into
   irregular chunks
1 x 400g tin of **cannellini beans**, drained
   and rinsed
salt and **black pepper**

METHOD

Scoop out the flesh of 1 of the avocados and add to a blender. Add the lime juice, half of the green chilli and the olive oil. Season well and blitz until smooth.

Cut the remaining avocado into chunks.

To assemble, toss together the avocado, cucumber, sugar snaps and cannellini beans in a bowl. Pour over the avocado dressing and garnish with the remaining green chilli slices and a drizzle of olive oil. Finish with a grind of black pepper.

TIME: 15 MINUTES   SERVES: 4   VEGAN, GLUTEN-FREE   93

Whipped Goat's Cheese + Carrots

THE DISH

A gnarly, honey-roasted carrot is undoubtedly the best type of carrot. The contrast between the sweetness of that veg with the sharp, tangy goat's cheese yoghurt and toasted walnuts in this dish is unbeatable, in our minds. If you can't get hold of Aleppo pepper, try using chilli flakes or smoked paprika instead.

INGREDIENTS

800g **carrots with tops**
olive oil, to drizzle
200g thick **Greek yoghurt** (we like
    Total Fage 5%)
125g **goat's cheese**
80g **walnuts**
4 tbsp **honey**
2 tsp **Aleppo pepper** or **chilli flakes**
salt

METHOD

Preheat the oven to 200°C fan.

Remove the tops from the carrots, saving a handful of them until later. Cut any very large carrots in half vertically, leaving smaller ones whole.

Pop the carrots onto a large baking tray. Drizzle with olive oil and a pinch of salt, then roast for 45 minutes, tossing every so often so that they cook evenly.

Meanwhile, roughly chop the reserved carrot tops. Set aside until later.

Add the yoghurt to a bowl along with the goat's cheese. Whisk until totally combined, then season to taste with salt.

Line a small baking tray with baking paper, add the walnuts, then drizzle with 2 tablespoons of honey. Bake for 12 minutes until fragrant and golden. Allow to cool slightly, and you'll get some crispy caramel-style bits.

Once the roasted carrots are gnarly and soft, add 1 teaspoon of Aleppo pepper and 1 tablespoon of honey to the tray and toss to coat.

To serve, swoosh around the goat's cheese mix on a serving plate. Place the carrots on top, along with the crispy caramelised walnuts. Drizzle with the remaining honey and sprinkle over the remaining Aleppo pepper and the reserved carrot tops. Finish with a drizzle of olive oil.

TIME: 1 HOUR   SERVES: 4   VEGGIE, GLUTEN-FREE

Prawn, Hispi + Kewpie Salad

THE DISH

Here's a salad that feels light and substantial at the same time. Kewpie is the secret to binding the ingredients together. If you're not already a Kewpie fanatic, all you need to know is that it's an easy-to-find Japanese mayonnaise that is intensely creamy and savoury. Pickled sushi ginger is another seriously slept-on ingredient that we've put to good use.

INGREDIENTS

olive oil, to fry
300g **raw king prawns**
1 **hispi cabbage** (also known as sweetheart or pointed cabbage in the supermarket), finely shredded
4 **spring onions**, finely sliced
60g **kewpie mayonnaise**
3 tbsp **pickled sushi ginger**, plus 4 tbsp pickling liquid
20g **roasted salted peanuts**, roughly chopped
salt and **black pepper**

METHOD

Set a frying pan over a medium heat, add a little olive oil, then fry the prawns in batches. They will curl and turn pink when cooked. Remove them from the pan, then set aside to cool.

Add the cabbage to a large bowl with a pinch of salt, then briefly massage it with your hands to soften it slightly. Season well.

Add the prawns to the bowl, along with most of the spring onions (hold back some greens to garnish). Add half of the kewpie mayo and 2 tablespoons of the sushi ginger pickling liquid. Toss the salad to combine.

Arrange the salad on a plate, then top with the sushi ginger, the reserved spring onions and the salted peanuts. In a small bowl, mix the remaining kewpie mayo and 2 tablespoons of the sushi ginger pickling liquid, then drizzle on top of the salad before serving with a grind of black pepper.

TIP

This looks prettiest with pink pickled sushi ginger, but don't worry if you can't find it.

Grated Tomatoes +
Beans with Anchovies

THE DISH

Grating tomatoes at the height of their season is a really lovely way of eating them. We've prepared them super simply and served them up with chubby white beans and some garlicky toast for dunking. Shout out to our friend Kitty Coles for the inspiration.

INGREDIENTS

6 large **tomatoes**, halved
2 tbsp **olive oil**, plus extra to fry
1 x 600g jar of **white beans**, drained
    and rinsed
4 slices of **sourdough**, sliced
1 **garlic clove**, halved
1 x 50g tin of **anchovy fillets in oil**, drained
a handful of **chives**, finely chopped
salt and **black pepper**

METHOD

Pop a box grater into a bowl. On the coarsest side of the grater, grate the tomatoes cut-side down, until you have just the skins remaining. Discard the skins.

Add a pinch of salt and 2 tablespoons of olive oil to the tomatoes, then mix. Tip in the beans, mix again, then leave to sit for a bit.

Set a frying pan over a high heat, then drizzle in a little olive oil. Add the sourdough and fry for a few minutes on each side until well toasted. Once toasted, rub the garlic halves all over the slices to infuse them with flavour.

Spoon the tomatoey beans into serving bowls, add plenty of black pepper, then top with the anchovies and chives. Serve with the garlicky toast for dunking.

SWAP

We like cannellini beans here, but any white bean would work.

TIME: 15 MINUTES   **SERVES: 4**   99

Courgette + Kale Salad

THE DISH

Get the most out of the humble courgette by using it in two very different ways. This salad is packed with charred chunks of courgette along with some really finely sliced discs. Great for meal prep or as a summery barbecue side.

INGREDIENTS

200g **bulgar wheat**
500g **courgettes**
3 tbsp **olive oil**, plus extra to drizzle
2 **lemons**, zested and juiced
250g **kale**, stalks discarded, leaves torn
150g **fresh pesto**
60g **Parmesan**, grated
salt and **black pepper**

METHOD

Cook the bulgar wheat according to the packet instructions. Drain and set aside.

While the bulgar is cooking, chop half of the courgettes into irregular chunks and add to a bowl with 2 tablespoons of olive oil, the juice of ½ a lemon and a pinch of salt. Toss to combine.

Set a large frying pan over a high heat and tip in the courgette chunks, frying for about 5 minutes until they char and tossing so that they cook evenly. Set aside to cool.

Finely slice the remaining courgettes with a mandoline, or a very sharp knife.

Pop the kale into a large bowl and add the juice of ½ a lemon, then add 1 tablespoon of olive oil and a pinch of salt. Massage the kale with your hands for about 5 minutes until the leaves look wet and bright green. They should drastically reduce in size.

Tip the charred and finely sliced courgettes into the kale bowl, along with the bulgar wheat, fresh pesto, the zest and remaining juice of the lemons, half of the grated Parmesan, a drizzle of olive oil and a pinch of salt. Toss to coat.

Arrange the salad on a platter, then top with the remaining Parmesan. Finish with plenty of black pepper.

TIME: 30 MINUTES **SERVES: 4**

Steak + Kohlrabi Lime Salad

THE DISH

Kohlrabi is a painfully underused vegetable – it tastes like a milder, sweeter version of a turnip and takes on the flavour of dressings in a slaw just wonderfully. Give it a go, you won't regret it.

INGREDIENTS

2 **rump steaks**
2 tbsp **fish sauce** (check the label if making gluten-free)
2 **limes**
2 tbsp **olive oil**, plus extra to fry
200g **sugar snap peas**, sliced in half lengthways
1 **kohlrabi** (approx. 250g), thinly sliced or cut into matchsticks
20g **roasted salted peanuts**, finely chopped
salt and **black pepper**

METHOD

Season the steaks with salt and drizzle over 1 tablespoon of fish sauce. Use your hands to rub in the fish sauce and set aside.

Add the rest of the fish sauce, the juice of 1½ limes and 2 tablespoons of olive oil to a bowl.

Add the sugar snaps and kohlrabi to the fish sauce and lime juice mixture.

Set a frying pan over a high heat. Drizzle olive oil over the steaks and rub in well.

Make sure the pan is really hot, before frying the steaks for 2 minutes on each side, until each has a nice golden crust. Set aside to rest on a chopping board for at least 5 minutes.

Slice the steak into thin strips, going against the grain.

Plate up the salad, serve the steak strips on top and scatter over the salted peanuts and a grind of black pepper. Serve with the remaining ½ lime to squeeze over.

Duck + No Pancakes

THE DISH

All the best bits of a takeaway (that's crispy duck and hoisin sauce to you and me) but a touch lighter. The spring greens are sautéed with five spice for that distinctive Peking duck flavour.

INGREDIENTS

2 **duck breasts** (approx. 175g each)
1½ tsp **five spice**
250g **spring greens**
4 tbsp **hoisin sauce**
½ **cucumber**, thinly sliced or cut into matchsticks
3 **spring onions**, thinly sliced or cut into matchsticks
salt

METHOD

Use a sharp knife to score a criss-cross grid into the fat of the duck skin, taking care not to cut through to the meat. Season generously with salt and a pinch of the five spice. Put the duck skin-side down into a cold frying pan, lay a small sheet of baking paper on top of the duck, then weigh the duck breasts down with another pan. This will ensure the duck has even contact with the pan and gets nice and crispy. Turn on the heat to medium-low and render the duck fat for 15 minutes until golden and crisp.

Meanwhile, thickly shred three-quarters of the spring greens, then very finely shred the remaining quarter.

Once the duck fat has rendered, flip the duck over and cook for a further 2–3 minutes, then remove from the pan and set aside to rest.

For the 'seaweed,' increase the heat to medium-high and fry the finely shredded spring greens in the duck fat – tilt the pan slightly so they collect in the corner and deep fry as much as possible. Fry for 1–2 minutes until crisp, then drain on a plate lined with a piece of kitchen paper. Season with a little sprinkle of the remaining five spice and a big pinch of salt. Set aside.

Throw the thickly shredded spring greens into the pan, add 2 tablespoons of water and the remaining five spice and sauté until wilted.

Cut the duck into 7–8 slices, against the grain. Collect any juices from the duck and pour into a bowl, then mix with the hoisin sauce. To serve, lay the duck on the bed of wilted greens and arrange the cucumber and spring onion strips on the side. Drizzle with the hoisin sauce and top with the crispy seaweed.

Herby Bread Salad

THE DISH

This salad thrives because of the marriage of three simple but delicious things: homemade breadcrumbs, lightly pickled shallots and a boatload of herbs. Your new go-to side salad.

INGREDIENTS

1 **shallot**, thinly sliced into rounds
4 tbsp **sherry vinegar** or **red wine vinegar**
100g stale, crustless **sourdough**
4 tbsp **extra virgin olive oil**
3 **baby gem lettuces**, quartered
a large handful of **flat leaf parsley** leaves
a large handful of **mint** leaves
salt and **black pepper**

METHOD

Separate the shallot rounds into rings with your thumb and add to a small bowl. Cover with sherry vinegar, season with a big pinch of salt and scrunch well with your hand to combine. Set aside to lightly pickle.

Blitz the sourdough in a food processor to make breadcrumbs or shred it by hand.

Set a large frying pan over a medium heat with 2 tablespoons of extra virgin olive oil and add the breadcrumbs. Fry for 3 minutes until deeply golden. Season well and set aside.

Arrange the baby gem quarters on a serving platter. Scatter over the herb leaves, then sprinkle over the pickled shallots, including their vinegar.

Finally, scatter over the toasted breadcrumbs, followed by the remaining 2 tablespoons of olive oil. Toss to serve.

Miso Mushroom Soba Soup

THE DISH

The texture of a fried mushroom is a plant-based marvel – it's got this lovely crispness and chewiness and, once it's tossed in a sticky sauce, you'll almost forget that it's a vegetable. You can eat these in loads of ways, but we've used them in this recipe as a nifty soup topper.

INGREDIENTS

400g **mixed mushrooms**
3 tbsp **cornflour**
3 tbsp **vegetable oil**
5 tbsp **white miso paste**
3 tbsp **agave**
200g **soba noodles**
4 **spring onions**, thinly sliced
salt

METHOD

Pour the mushrooms into a large bowl. Sprinkle over the cornflour and a pinch of salt, then toss so they are totally coated.

Heat a frying pan over a high heat and add the vegetable oil. Add your mushrooms a few at a time and fry for a couple of minutes on each side until crisp, then lay them on a baking tray or plate lined with kitchen paper. Repeat until all your mushrooms are golden.

Add 3 tablespoons of the miso paste to the same frying pan along with the agave and 2 tablespoons of water. Bring to a very gentle simmer, then remove from the heat.

Cook the soba noodles according to the packet instructions, then rinse with cold water and set aside.

Add the mushrooms to the pan of miso sauce, then gently simmer for 2 minutes to heat through. The cornflour will help to thicken the sauce.

Add the remaining 2 tablespoons of miso paste to a heatproof jug, then pour over 1 litre of boiling water. Whisk to combine.

Divide the noodles between 4 bowls. Pour over the miso soup, then top with the crispy mushrooms and spring onions before serving.

TIME: 30 MINUTES   SERVES: 4   VEGAN, GLUTEN-FREE   109

Roasted Grape + Chicken Salad

THE DISH

Roasting grapes makes them incredibly sweet and concentrated in flavour – plus, you're left with lots of delicious caramelised grape juice in the pan. Combining those grapes with crisp, juicy chicken and chicken-fat croutons makes for a mega eating experience.

INGREDIENTS

4 skin-on, boneless **chicken thighs**
100g stale, crustless **sourdough**, torn into rough croutons
300g **red grapes**
2 tbsp **lemon juice**
4 tbsp **extra virgin olive oil**
1 bag of **salad mix**
100g rindless **goat's cheese**
salt and **black pepper**

METHOD

Preheat the oven to 180°C fan. Season the chicken with salt and pepper all over. Lay the chicken thighs on a baking tray, skin-side down, and place a sheet of baking paper over them, then another baking tray on top. This will keep the skin in contact with the tray and help the fat to render out. Roast for 20 minutes until the base tray has lots of golden chicken fat and juices.

Remove the upper tray from the chicken and flip the chicken thighs over. Toss the sourdough croutons in the chicken fat and juices, and season again with salt and pepper. Nestle the grapes into the tray and return to the oven for a further 20 minutes until the chicken thighs are golden and the grapes have wilted and burst. There will be sticky grape juice caramelised in pools on the tray and the croutons should be golden and crisp.

Meanwhile, whisk together the lemon juice and olive oil with a big pinch of salt and pepper until thickened into a dressing.

When the chicken, croutons and grapes are cooked, remove from the tray, scraping as much of the sticky goodness from the bottom of the tray as you can. Transfer the grapes and croutons into a large salad bowl. Slice the chicken and add to the bowl with the salad leaves. Crumble in the goat's cheese and toss with the dressing, getting your hands in there to make sure everything is generously coated.

SWAP

If you're not a fan of goat's cheese, try Taleggio or Gorgonzola.

TIME: 45 MINUTES   SERVES: 2

Pesto Lentils
with Lemony Leeks

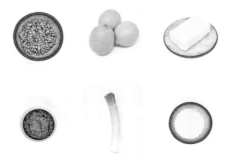

THE DISH

An easy way to make something as simple as a lentil feel indulgent. We've cooked up our green lentils with a little butter, stirred through some pesto and topped them with lemony leeks. Perfect as a side dish or part of a champion mezze.

INGREDIENTS

500g **tinned green lentils**, drained and rinsed
1 **lemon**, zested and juiced, plus extra wedges
   to serve
50g **salted butter**
1 jar of **pesto**
4 **leeks**, halved lengthways
4 tbsp **olive oil**
50g **panko breadcrumbs**
salt

METHOD

Set a saucepan over a medium heat. Add the lentils and 50ml of water and bring to a simmer. Turn off the heat and add the lemon zest, butter and two-thirds of the pesto and stir to combine. Set aside.

Set a griddle pan over a high heat and add the leeks, cut-side down. Cook for about 5 minutes on each side until charred and soft.

Set a small frying pan over a high heat and add 2 tablespoons of olive oil and the breadcrumbs, toasting until golden brown. Toss with a pinch of salt.

Remove the leeks from the heat and dress generously with the lemon juice, salt and remaining olive oil.

Put the lentils onto a platter and swirl in the remaining pesto. Top with the charred leeks, sprinkle over the breadcrumbs and serve with extra lemon wedges.

TIME: 20 MINUTES   **SERVES: 4**   **VEGGIE   113**

'Nduja Honey Aubergines + Labneh

THE DISH

'Nduja and honey are the best of pals. The sweetness of honey offsets the heat of 'nduja in the most magical way. We've drizzled it over thick lemony yoghurt and fat coins of aubergine. We won't judge you for licking the plate clean.

INGREDIENTS

2 **aubergines**, sliced into 2cm-thick rounds
4 tbsp **olive oil**
450g thick **Greek yoghurt** (we like
   Total Fage 5%)
1 **lemon**
4 tbsp **'nduja**
4 tbsp **honey**
2 **flatbreads**, to serve
salt and **black pepper**

METHOD

Preheat the oven to 200°C fan.

Arrange the aubergines on 1 large baking tray, or 2 smaller ones. Drizzle with a generous glug of olive oil and a big pinch of salt, toss to coat, then roast for 40 minutes, flipping halfway through.

Meanwhile, put the yoghurt in a bowl and add the zest and juice of ½ a lemon and a big pinch of salt. Give it a good mix, then tip the yoghurt out into a clean tea towel (or clean, new J-Cloth). Gather the top of the tea towel and twist it. Pop it in a sieve set over a bowl, then leave to sit.

Once the aubergines are tender, remove them from the oven.

Add 3 tablespoons of olive oil to a frying pan set over a medium heat, then add the 'nduja. Cook gently for a few minutes until the 'nduja has broken down and the oil is tinged red. Add the honey and cook until it loosens up. Remove the pan from the heat.

Cut the remaining lemon half into wedges. Swoosh the labneh around on a serving plate, then top with the aubergines. Spoon over the 'nduja honey, then serve with the lemon wedges and flatbreads for scooping. Finish with a grind of black pepper.

Harissa + Caper Giant Couscous

THE DISH

Giant couscous is so much heartier than its more diminutive cousin. It's got a nice bit of bite, and it's so satisfying to eat. Butternut squash lends a pleasant thump of sweetness to this spicy dish. We suggest making double the amount of crispy capers – they're that crunchy and addictive.

INGREDIENTS

1 **butternut squash** (approx. 900g), cut into 2½cm chunks, no need to peel
2 **aubergines**, cut into 2½cm chunks
90g **harissa**
10 tbsp **extra virgin olive oil**, plus extra to drizzle
150g **capers**
a small handful of **flat leaf parsley**, stalks and leaves kept separate, finely chopped
250g **giant couscous**
salt

METHOD

Preheat the oven to 180°C fan.

Put the butternut squash and aubergines on 2 large baking trays.

Mix together the harissa and 4 tablespoons of extra virgin olive oil in a bowl. Divide the mixture evenly between the baking trays to coat the vegetables.

Roast for 45 minutes until soft and caramelised, swapping shelves halfway through to ensure even cooking.

Drain the capers and pat them dry with kitchen paper. Add the remaining 6 tablespoons of olive oil to a small frying pan set over a low heat. Add the capers and parsley stalks and fry until crisp, around 3 minutes – the capers will butterfly open. Use a slotted spoon to remove them from the oil and drain on kitchen paper.

Set a large saucepan of salted water over a medium-high heat to boil and pour in the couscous. Boil for 10 minutes until al dente, then drain and rinse under cold water to remove the excess starch. Toss through most of the chopped parsley leaves.

Top the couscous with the roasted veg, the crispy caper mixture and remaining parsley leaves, drizzle with olive oil and serve.

Celeriac Pomodoro

THE DISH

Okay, we know it's not 2012 and people aren't really spiralizing anymore, but using celeriac as a sort-of tagliatelle substitute gives this plate an incredible earthiness while still being fresher and lighter than pasta and technically one of your five-a-day. A big win from us, inspired by a lovely Jane Baxter recipe.

INGREDIENTS

3 tbsp **extra virgin olive oil**, plus extra
    to drizzle
4 **garlic cloves**, thinly sliced
1 x 400g tin of **plum tomatoes**
1 small **celeriac**, peeled (approx. 600g)
1 tbsp **balsamic vinegar**
30g **Parmesan**, grated
a small handful of **flat leaf parsley** leaves,
    finely chopped
salt and **black pepper**

METHOD

Set a frying pan over a medium heat, add 3 tablespoons of the oil and the garlic and cook until fragrant – the garlic will be wiggling around in the pan, but we don't want it to get any colour.

Add the tomatoes, bashing with a wooden spoon to break them up, then add a tinful of water. Bring to a boil, then reduce the heat to a simmer. Season well and let the sauce reduce for 15–20 minutes.

Meanwhile, slice the celeriac very thinly using a mandoline or a sharp knife, then cut into strips around the same thickness as tagliatelle – they won't be as long, but don't worry.

Once the sauce has reduced, add the balsamic vinegar and season to taste.

Set a large saucepan of salted water over a medium-high heat and bring to a boil. Add the celeriac and cook for 3–4 minutes until tender and al dente – take care not to overcook or it will become a bit mushy.

Drain the celeriac and add to the sauce, tossing gently to combine. Drizzle with olive oil and serve scattered with the Parmesan and parsley.

TIME: 30 MINUTES   **SERVES: 2**   **GLUTEN-FREE**   119

Curried Cauliflower Soup

THE DISH

We love a hearty soup with a crispy topping, and this curried cauli number is fast becoming a favourite. This recipe makes a big batch, and freezes well in airtight containers, where it will last for up to three months. If you don't want to turn on your oven, you can poach the cauliflower in the soup and blend it up once the cauliflower is tender.

INGREDIENTS

2 large **cauliflowers**, broken into
   bite-sized florets, stalks roughly
   chopped, leaves reserved
olive oil
4 **shallots**, sliced into rounds
vegetable oil, to fry
5 tbsp **korma curry paste** (check the label
   if making gluten-free)
1 x 400ml tin of **coconut milk**
3 tbsp **lime pickle** or **mango chutney**
a handful of **coriander** leaves
salt and **black pepper**

METHOD

Preheat the oven to 220°C fan. Add the cauliflower florets and stalks to a couple of large baking trays, drizzle with olive oil and a good pinch of salt, then roast for 40 minutes.

Set a large saucepan (it needs to fit all the soup and cauliflower in it) over a medium heat. Add three-quarters of the shallots and a splash of olive oil and cook for 15 minutes until totally softened and starting to caramelise.

Set a small pan over a low heat, add a generous amount of vegetable oil and add the remaining shallots, then allow to come up to heat gently. Once the oil is sizzling, cook for 5 minutes until the shallots are golden and crisp. Remove from the pan with a slotted spoon, then leave to cool on a plate lined with kitchen paper.

Add the curry paste to the large saucepan of shallots and cook for 3 minutes until the oil separates and it smells fragrant. Add the coconut milk, 2½ tablespoons of lime pickle and 1 litre of water, then simmer for 5 minutes.

Once the cauliflower florets and stalks are totally tender with lovely caramelised edges, add them to the large saucepan. Simmer for another 5 minutes, then use a stick blender to blitz in the pan until smooth. Season to taste.

Reduce the oven to 200°C fan. Add the leaves to the large baking trays, drizzle with olive oil and salt and bake for 5–8 minutes until crisp. Meanwhile, mix the remaining lime pickle in a bowl with water to form a drizzle.

Spoon the soup into bowls. Top with the roasted cauliflower leaves, crispy shallots and coriander leaves, with a drizzle of the lime pickle mixture to serve. Finish with a grind of black pepper.

Crispy Spring Gnocchi

THE DISH

We were inspired to make this delightful combo by the clever clogs over at London's Forza Wine. Shaved raw courgettes and asparagus are so crunchy and fresh. And you won't believe how much flavour deeply roasted hazelnuts can bring to this simple bit of cooking.

INGREDIENTS

50g **hazelnuts**
4 tbsp **extra virgin olive oil**
300g **gnocchi**
1 **courgette**, thinly sliced or shaved
200g **asparagus**, thinly sliced or shaved
1 **lemon**, zested and juiced
20g **Parmesan**, finely grated
salt and **black pepper**

METHOD

Preheat the oven to 180°C fan.

Pop the hazelnuts on a baking tray and roast for 10 minutes until deeply brown and smelling very nutty. Alternatively, toast them in a dry frying pan. Finely chop the nuts and set aside.

Set a frying pan over a medium-high heat and add 2 tablespoons of the olive oil and the gnocchi. Fry for 3–4 minutes until golden on all sides and crisp.

Meanwhile, add most of the hazelnuts, the courgette, asparagus, lemon zest and juice and the remaining olive oil to a large bowl. Season generously and toss through half of the Parmesan.

Add the crispy gnocchi to the bowl and toss well to combine. Serve garnished with the remaining Parmesan and hazelnuts.

SWAP

Switch up the veg here depending on the time of year – it would also be lovely with kale and Jerusalem artichokes in winter.

TIME: 20 MINUTES   **SERVES: 2**

Orange + Feta Quinoa Salad

THE DISH

Pre-cooked grain pouches are a lifesaver and the quinoa in this recipe absorbs so much of the lovely citrussy dressing. Paired with zingy orange segments and some spiced, crispy chickpeas, this is a stunning winter salad.

INGREDIENTS

2 x 400g tins of **chickpeas**, drained and rinsed
110ml **olive oil**, plus extra to drizzle
2 tbsp **hot smoked paprika**, plus extra to garnish
6 **oranges**
2 x 250g pouches of **quinoa**
a large handful of **mint**, leaves picked
200g **feta**
salt and **black pepper**

METHOD

Preheat the oven to 200°C fan.

Pat the chickpeas dry with kitchen paper and tip into a roasting tin, then drizzle over 2 tablespoons of olive oil, the paprika and a large pinch of salt. Toss to combine, then bake for 25 minutes until crisp, tossing occasionally so that they cook evenly. Set aside to cool.

Cut the tops and bottoms off the oranges to create flat surfaces. Stand an orange on one of the flat ends, then shave off the skin with a small, serrated knife. Remove any excess pith, too. Repeat for all of the oranges.

Cut along the inside edges of each segment to release them, then set aside.

Squeeze any excess juice from the orange middles into a bowl. Add 90ml of olive oil, then season to taste with salt and pepper.

Pop the quinoa into a large bowl, then add the roasted chickpeas, orange segments, mint leaves and orange dressing. Crumble in the feta in large chunks. Toss to combine.

Arrange the salad on plates, then sprinkle with a little more paprika and a drizzle of olive oil.

SWAP

Swap the quinoa for giant couscous for a chewy, hearty meal.

TIME: 35 MINUTES   SERVES: 4

Sausage + Porcini Paccheri

THE DISH

Sausage pasta is just about the most comforting food out there. The method for this one is really simple. We use porcini mushrooms for savoury funk and Parmesan to get it nice and creamy. If you can't get your hands on paccheri, use any large tube-shaped pasta such as rigatoni.

INGREDIENTS

40g **dried porcini mushrooms**
6 **sausages**, meat squeezed out
1 tbsp **olive oil**, if needed
500g **paccheri**
2 **garlic cloves**, finely chopped
a handful of **thyme** leaves, plus extra sprigs
   to garnish
120g **Parmesan**, grated
salt

METHOD

Add the mushrooms to a heatproof jug, then pour over 250ml of boiling water. Leave to sit for 10–15 minutes. Remove the mushrooms from their liquid with a slotted spoon (reserving the liquid) and finely chop.

Meanwhile, set a frying pan over a medium-high heat. Add the sausage meat and let it sizzle and fry until golden, breaking up the chunks with the side of a wooden spoon to form a crisp, brown mince – you may need a glug of oil to help. Remove from the pan, leaving the fat behind.

Set a saucepan of salted water over a medium heat and bring to a boil. Add the paccheri and cook for 8–10 minutes until al dente.

Reduce the heat to low under the frying pan that held the sausages, then add the garlic, thyme and porcini. Cook for a minute until fragrant. Pour in the porcini mushroom liquid. Reduce by half, then add the sausage meat and most of the Parmesan. Let the Parmesan melt to form a thick sauce.

Once the pasta has cooked, add some pasta water to the frying pan. Lift the pasta straight from its cooking water into the sauce. Give it a good mix, adding more pasta water to bring it all together to a glossy sauce. Add more Parmesan and thyme sprigs before serving.

TIP

Get the best-quality pork sausages you can – it's much easier to squeeze them out of their skins, and they're packed with flavour.

TIME: 30 MINUTES   SERVES: 4   129

Preserved Lemon + Prawn Linguine

THE DISH

Prawn, lemon and chilli are a classic combo. Using preserved lemon here makes the whole dish more aromatic and fragrant. It's a simple way to add an extra punch of depth without sacrificing that citrus freshness.

INGREDIENTS

160–200g **linguine**
3 tbsp **extra virgin olive oil**
300g **cherry tomatoes**
1 **red chilli**, finely chopped
25g **flat leaf parsley**, stalks finely chopped, leaves roughly chopped
2 **preserved lemons**, rind finely chopped, inner flesh discarded
200g **raw king prawns**
salt and **black pepper**

METHOD

Set a large saucepan of salted water over a medium heat and bring to a boil. Add the pasta and cook for 8–10 minutes until al dente.

Meanwhile, set a cast iron pan over a high heat and add 1 tablespoon of olive oil and the tomatoes, frying until charred and blackened in places. Set aside.

Drizzle the remaining 2 tablespoons of olive oil into a large frying pan and set over a medium heat. Add the red chilli and parsley stalks and fry for a couple of minutes before adding in half of the preserved lemon, the prawns and the charred tomatoes. Cook for around 2 minutes until the prawns have turned pink, then set aside.

Once the pasta has cooked, reserve a mugful of the starchy pasta water before draining the pasta and adding it to the frying pan.

Add the parsley leaves to the frying pan, along with as much of the reserved pasta water as you need to make a silky sauce. Shake the pan until the sauce has thickened.

Season, then serve with the remaining preserved lemon.

TIME: 20 MINUTES   **SERVES: 2**

Kimchi + Pancetta Fettuccine

THE DISH

If you want a speedy and hearty weeknight dinner, this is it. Pancetta, blistered tomatoes, Parmesan and garlic are tossed together with fettuccine, but it's the kimchi that's the star of the show. Cooking your kimchi turns down the volume on its signature funk and adds a mellow warmth to the whole dish. An icon.

INGREDIENTS

300g **pancetta lardons**
1 tbsp **olive oil**
400g **fettuccine**
3 **garlic cloves**, finely chopped or grated
300g **kimchi**, chopped
500g **mixed cherry vine tomatoes**
30g **Parmesan**, finely grated, plus extra
 to serve
salt and **black pepper**

METHOD

Set a frying pan over a medium heat and fry the pancetta with the olive oil until the fat has rendered and the pancetta is crispy. Remove with a slotted spoon and set aside, keeping the fat in the pan.

Meanwhile, set a large saucepan of salted water over a medium heat and bring to a boil. Add the pasta and cook for 8–10 minutes until al dente, then drain, reserving a mugful of the starchy pasta water for later.

Set the frying pan with the pancetta fat over a medium-low heat, add the garlic and kimchi and fry for 1 minute until fragrant. Throw in the tomatoes and cook, stirring regularly, until the tomatoes burst and become jammy, about 6 minutes.

Add the Parmesan and most of the pancetta and follow with the pasta. Toss well to coat, adding the reserved pasta water to loosen the sauce and make it glossy. Season to taste with salt and pepper.

Top each plate of pasta with the reserved crispy pancetta and more Parmesan.

TIP

It's not totally necessary to use mixed cherry vine tomatoes, but they look so pretty!

TIME: 25 MINUTES

SERVES: 4

Peanut + Ginger 'Romesco' Udon

THE DISH

Peanuts, pickled ginger and roasted pepper join forces for a fragrant take on a classic romesco sauce. Thai basil is a must here for an extra aniseed kick.

INGREDIENTS

1 x 450g jar of **roasted red peppers**, drained
200g **roasted salted peanuts**, crushed
105g **pickled ginger**, plus 30ml pickling liquid
4 tbsp **olive oil**
10 **spring onions**
700g **fresh udon noodles**
a bunch of **Thai basil** leaves
salt

METHOD

Add the red peppers, 160g of peanuts, 90g of pickled ginger and the 30ml pickling liquid to a food processor. Blitz together, slowly trickling in 3 tablespoons of olive oil as you blend. Season with salt and set aside.

Heat a griddle pan over a high heat. Toss 8 of the spring onions with a little olive oil and salt, then cook until charred, sweet and tender. Finely chop the remaining 2 spring onions.

Cook the noodles according to the packet instructions, reserving some of the drained cooking water.

Toss the noodles with the romesco sauce, some of the cooking water, a handful of basil and the finely chopped raw spring onions.

Divide between 4 warm bowls and top each with a couple of the grilled spring onions, some extra basil, the remaining pickled ginger and crushed peanuts.

TIME: 15 MINUTES   **SERVES: 4**   **VEGAN**

6 Noodles You Need to Know

Walk into any decent supermarket nowadays and you're likely to be greeted by a wonderful and diverse range of noodles to choose from. You might be of the belief that a noodle's a noodle, but it's important to consider the texture, flavour and characteristics of each noodle before deciding on what kind you're going to use in a recipe. A few of them can be interchangeable, but we thought we'd give you the low-down on the most common types of noodles you'll encounter.

1. EGG NOODLES

Also known as lo mein, this very popular Chinese noodle is made from a combination of wheat flour and egg and is the most similar to pasta of all these noodles. You can typically buy them dried, fresh or 'straight-to-wok'. If dried or fresh, they usually need to be boiled before being stir-fried. Egg noodles have a pleasantly soft and spongy texture that holds up well with bold thick sauces and are sturdy enough to be pan-fried fairly aggressively – perfect for an oyster-sauce-heavy chicken noodle dish with plenty of beansprouts for added crunch.

2. RAMEN NOODLES

Ramen noodles are a Japanese noodle made from wheat, water and kansui (an alkaline mineral water). They are thin, springy and most often eaten in some sort of broth. Instant ramen noodles are quite different to traditional ramen noodles due to the flash-frying process used to preserve them. That process causes the dough to expand rapidly and is what creates instant ramen's signature curly shape. While regular ramen noodles tend to be paired with rich stocks and ingredients like nori and spring onions, instant ramen often come paired with relatively artificial and majorly delicious seasoning packets. One of our favourite things to do with an instant ramen packet is to whack a fried egg on top alongside a heap of grated cheese – it's so wrong, and so, so right.

3. RICE NOODLES

Rice noodles are made from rice flour and water. Go figure. A gluten-free staple, they come in both thin vermicelli style and flat, wide rice noodles. Rice noodles are used in all sorts of dishes like pho, laksa and summer rolls. They're soft, silky and don't have a long cooking time – all you need to do is soak them in boiling water until they're good to go. The mild flavour of these noods means they take on spice very well and can always benefit from a whack of fresh herbs and vegetables to liven them up. You always want to have a bit more sauce or dressing than you think with these. Our go-to rice noodle dressing is a 3:2:1 ratio of lime juice to fish sauce to tamarind paste, with a pinch of sugar.

4. UDON NOODLES

These are the thickest noodles in this line-up, and have a delightfully chewy, bouncy texture. Udon noodles are often served in a broth or stir-fried with other ingredients. They can be found fresh, frozen or dried – word to the wise: if you can find the fresh stuff, it's miles better than the rest. You'll be chuffed to hear that udon are a very popular hangover cure in Japan, so try putting aside the hash browns the next time you're hanging and give a big old bowl of udon a whirl for its restorative properties. We really like to eat our udon in a punchy gingery and garlicky broth with a frankly dangerous amount of chilli sauce. It's one hell of a way to start the day.

5. SOBA NOODLES

Soba noodles are another type of Japanese noodle traditionally made from buckwheat flour and wheat flour – they are thin, brown and have a deliciously nutty flavour. Soba are great eaten hot or cold and are considered one of the healthiest noodle choices due to being packed with fibre and protein. There's a common phrase in Japan that roughly translates to 'eat soba, live long' and we're absolutely here for it. Soba noodles really come to life when paired with quite delicate ingredients. Serve them in a sesame-oil-spiked vegetable broth with mushrooms and spring onions for a beautifully simple supper.

6. GLASS NOODLES

Glass noodles – also known as cellophane noodles – are easy to spot thanks to their see-through aesthetic. They might be transparent but these slurpable noodles can be made from any number of starches that aren't wheat or rice. Typically, that starch will come from something like sweet potato, potato or mung bean. Glass noodles are super thin, really delicate and have a slightly chewy texture when cooked. You'll find them in dishes like pad Thai and japchae, and used as a filling in spring rolls and dumplings. Glass noodles thrive when paired with both crunchy and soft additions – think beautifully tender beef or shredded peppers and carrots that haven't gone mushy – with plenty of soy sauce and brown sugar.

Chorizo Mac + Manchego

THE DISH

Say hello to your new favourite mac 'n' cheese. Manchego has a tangy, nutty and slightly sweet flavour that forms the backbone of an incredible sauce. You'll never look at Cheddar the same way again.

INGREDIENTS

300g **macaroni**
6 **cooking chorizo sausages**, skins removed, finely diced
3 tbsp **unsalted butter**
3 tbsp **plain flour**
500ml **whole milk**
200g **Manchego**, grated
salt and **black pepper**

METHOD

Set a large saucepan of salted water over a medium heat and bring to a boil. Cook the pasta for 2 minutes less than the packet instructions, then drain in a colander and refresh under a cool running tap to stop the pasta from cooking further. Set aside.

In a large saucepan, fry three-quarters of the diced chorizo sausage until cooked through and starting to crisp and the red oil has been released. Scrape the sausage out of the pan into a bowl and set aside.

Add the butter to the same pan and melt over a medium-low heat. Add the flour and whisk together to form a paste. Cook this for a minute until bubbly. Gradually add in the milk, whisking well after each addition until you have a smooth, lump-free sauce. Allow to simmer for 2 minutes to cook out the flour.

Turn off the heat and add most of the cheese, reserving a handful to sprinkle on top.

Put the pasta into an ovenproof dish and pour over the cheesy sauce. Add the cooked chorizo and stir through. Give a good grind of black pepper and season with salt.

Preheat the grill to its highest setting.

Sprinkle the remaining chorizo and cheese over the pasta and grill for 5 minutes until golden and bubbly.

TIME: 45 MINUTES   SERVES: 4

Pâté Pasta

THE DISH

Pâté might not be a store cupboard staple for everyone out there, but this is definitely a good recipe for that oddly specific part of the festive period where you find yourself with a tub of the stuff knocking around in the fridge but simply cannot bear to eat any more crackers.

INGREDIENTS

1 tbsp **extra virgin olive oil**, plus extra
   to drizzle
2 large **red onions** (approx. 300g),
   thinly sliced
60ml **sherry vinegar**
200g **pappardelle** or **mafalde**
80g **chicken liver pâté**
a small handful of **flat leaf parsley**,
   roughly chopped
2 tbsp **Parmesan**, grated
salt and **black pepper**

METHOD

Set a heavy frying pan over a medium-low heat and add the oil, onions and a big pinch of salt. Cook, stirring regularly and adding a splash of water from time to time, until the onions have softened significantly, taken on a deep purple colour and reduced by more than half in volume – this can take up to 30 minutes.

Once reduced and caramelised, add the vinegar and let it bubble away until almost no liquid remains in the pan.

Meanwhile, set a large saucepan of salted water over a medium heat and bring to a boil. Add the pasta and cook for 8–10 minutes until al dente.

Once cooked, transfer the pasta straight into the onion pan with the chicken liver pâté and toss vigorously to combine, adding pasta water as necessary to loosen and create a silky sauce. Season generously.

Serve drizzled with olive oil and sprinkled with the parsley and Parmesan.

TIME: 40 MINUTES   **SERVES: 2**   141

Sun-Dried Tomato + Porcini Pasta

THE DISH

You will not believe the amount of flavour we've put into this dish. Cooking the pasta in the porcini liquid is an easy win but make sure you remove it all with a slotted spoon to avoid ingesting any grit from the mushrooms at the bottom. No one likes grit in their dinner.

INGREDIENTS

30g **dried porcini mushrooms**
280g **sun-dried tomatoes in oil**, plus
   3 tbsp oil
300g **gemelli** or **fusilli**
1 tbsp **extra virgin olive oil**
2 **banana shallots**, finely diced
3 **garlic cloves**, finely diced or grated
30g **flat leaf parsley**, stalks finely chopped,
   leaves roughly chopped
salt

METHOD

Add the porcini mushrooms to a large saucepan. Cover with 1½ litres freshly boiled water, then leave for 20 minutes to soften.

Meanwhile, blitz half of the sun-dried tomatoes in a food processor along with 3 tablespoons of their oil until you have a rough paste. Roughly chop the remaining sun-dried tomatoes.

After 20 minutes, remove the mushrooms from their liquid and set aside. Set the saucepan of liquid over a high heat and bring to a boil. Add the pasta and cook for 8–10 minutes until al dente.

Set a frying pan over a medium heat and add the olive oil, the shallots and a big pinch of salt. Sweat for 5 minutes until translucent. Add the garlic and parsley stalks and cook for a further minute until fragrant.

Add the sun-dried tomato paste and cook over a low heat for 8–10 minutes until it has a deep, brick-red colour.

When the pasta has cooked, use a slotted spoon to add the pasta straight into the frying pan. Add the reserved porcini mushrooms and the remaining sun-dried tomatoes and toss well to coat, using as much porcini pasta water as you need to make a silky pasta sauce.

Stir through the parsley leaves, then plate up to serve.

Pesto Lasagne

THE DISH

This style of lasagne made with pesto comes from Liguria. Using shop-bought pesto means that a simplified version comes together quickly and easily. Expect fragrant basil and creamy béchamel. It's basically grown-up pesto pasta. Need we say more?

INGREDIENTS

75g **salted butter**
75g **plain flour**
1 litre **whole milk**
300g **fresh pesto**
60g **Parmesan**, grated
250g **fresh lasagne sheets**
salt and **black pepper**

METHOD

Preheat the oven to 200°C fan.

Firstly, make the roux that will become the base of the béchamel. Melt the butter in a large saucepan over a medium heat. Once bubbling, add the flour a spoonful at a time, whisking constantly.

When all the flour has been added and formed clumps, keep cooking and whisking for a minute to cook the flour slightly – it should be bubbling and nearly golden.

Now add the milk slowly, gradually whisking all the time so you don't get lumps. Once all the milk has been added, cook the sauce until it thickens to the consistency of double cream. Turn off the heat and season generously with salt and pepper.

Spread the base of an ovenproof dish with a thin layer of béchamel, 1–2 tablespoons of pesto and a hefty sprinkling of cheese, then top with a layer of pasta sheets. Repeat this process until you've used up everything – ending with an extra thick layer of béchamel and cheese on top.

Pop into the oven for 20 minutes until it is golden and bubbling. Allow the lasagne to rest for 5 minutes before serving. Finish with a grind of black pepper.

TIME: 35 MINUTES   **SERVES: 4**   145

Hoisin Tofu Noodles

METHOD

Set a saucepan of water over a medium heat and bring to a boil. Cook the rice noodles according to the packet instructions and, when ready, rinse with cold water and set aside in a colander.

Set a wok over a medium heat. Add 1 tablespoon of oil, then tip in the spring onions. Fry for a few minutes until they are softened, then remove from the wok and set aside until later.

Add the remaining 3 tablespoons of oil to the wok. Crumble the tofu directly into the wok, creating small mince-like pieces. Increase the heat and fry for 5 minutes until the tofu is golden and crispy. Add the garlic, chilli and 2 tablespoons of hoisin sauce, then toss to coat.

In a bowl, mix the remaining 4 tablespoons of hoisin sauce with 2 tablespoons of water to loosen it up a bit.

Tip the noodles into the wok along with the spring onions and the hoisin sauce. Toss with tongs until the noodles are totally mixed in with the tofu.

Season to taste with salt and pepper, then serve up.

THE DISH

Speedy noodle dishes are a great midweek staple to have under your belt. Crumbling tofu into a hot frying pan like this gets it super crispy and mimics the texture of mince. No, really. Tossed around with hoisin sauce, these noodles are an umami and protein-packed dinner.

INGREDIENTS

200g **rice noodles**
4 tbsp **vegetable oil**
6 **spring onions**, cut into 2cm lengths
450g **firm tofu**, drained and patted dry
2 **garlic cloves**, finely chopped
2 **red chillies**, finely chopped
6 tbsp **hoisin sauce** (check the label if making gluten-free)
salt and **black pepper**

TIME: 20 MINUTES   SERVES: 4   VEGAN, GLUTEN-FREE

Aubergine Gochujang Noodles

THE DISH

Zhuzhing up instant noodles is a favourite pastime of ours. These creamy, spicy and salty noodles make the perfect quick vegan supper – you can also swap the aubergine for any leftover cooked veg that need to be used up.

INGREDIENTS

1 **aubergine**, cut into 2cm chunks
2 tbsp **vegetable oil**
2 tbsp **soy sauce**
2 tbsp **gochujang paste**
2 tbsp **peanut butter**
2 packets of **vegan instant ramen**
1 **spring onion**, thinly sliced

METHOD

Preheat the oven to 180°C fan.

Line a baking tray with baking paper. Toss the aubergines in a bowl with the oil, spread out on the baking tray and roast for 20 minutes. Remove from the oven and pour over the soy sauce, tossing well to coat. Return to the oven for 15 minutes until the aubergine is tender, sticky and caramelised. If it looks a little dry and overdone, add a splash of water to the tray to help you get it saucy and coated again.

In a small bowl, whisk together the gochujang, peanut butter and ramen seasoning packets with 3 tablespoons of water. Set aside.

Set a large saucepan of water over a medium heat and bring to a boil. Cook the ramen for 3–4 minutes until tender. Drain in a colander, then add back to the pan and pour in the gochujang mixture. Stir well to combine.

Serve the noodles topped with the sticky soy aubergine and spring onion to garnish.

TIME: 40 MINUTES **SERVES: 2** **VEGAN** 151

Crab + Tomato Pici

THE DISH

Pici is a beautiful pasta and has a unique chew that's immeasurably satisfying. It's also probably the easiest pasta to make by hand. There are no machines required in this recipe, all you need is a bowl and your bare hands – and, hey, why not get your guests involved with the rolling as well?

INGREDIENTS

375g **'00' flour** or **strong white bread flour**
2 tbsp **olive oil**, plus extra to fry
400g **Datterini tomatoes**, halved
1 tbsp **red miso**
200g **mixed crab**
a handful of **tarragon**, leaves picked
1 **lemon**, juiced
salt and **black pepper**

SWAP

You can use cherry or baby plum tomatoes instead of Datterini, but you may need to add a bit of water to help them release their juices.

METHOD

Combine the flour with 180ml of water in a bowl. Add 2 tablespoons of olive oil and a big pinch of salt. Mix into a shaggy dough, turn out onto a clean work surface and knead for 5–6 minutes until smooth and elastic. Cover and rest for 30 minutes.

While the dough is resting, set a large frying pan over a high heat and cover the base with olive oil. When the pan is very hot, add the tomatoes with a big pinch of salt. Cook over a high heat, stirring and scraping the bottom of the pan regularly, until the tomatoes are very, very reduced and the olive oil has split out of the mix. If the tomatoes start to catch too soon you may need to add a splash of water. Stir in the miso and keep warm.

To make the pici, make sure your work surface is free of any flour. Cut the rested dough ball into 16 roughly equal pieces, then cut each piece into 3 lengths. Using both hands, roll each piece into a rope about 30cm long and just under ½cm thick. Lightly flour the pici.

Set a large saucepan of generously salted water over a medium heat and bring to a boil. Drop the pici into the water and cook for 3–4 minutes until they float to the surface. Reserve a mugful of starchy pasta water for later. Drain the pici in a colander.

Toss the pasta into the sauce until it is coated, adding some pasta water to loosen if you need to. Add the crab and tarragon, saving some for garnish, and stir through.

Finish with some lemon juice to taste and season with salt and black pepper. Divide between warm bowls and get stuck in.

EASY EVENINGS   EASY EVENINGS

EASY EVENINGS

SY EVENINGS

EASY EVENINGS

ASY EVENINGS   05. EASY EVENINGS

EASY EVENINGS

SY EVENINGS

EASY EVENINGS

ASY EVENINGS   05. EASY EVENINGS

EASY EVENINGS

SY EVENINGS

EASY EVENINGS

SY EVENINGS   05. EASY EVENINGS

EASY EVENINGS

EASY EVENING

EASY EVENINGS

05. EASY EVENINGS 05. EASY EVENIN

EASY EVENINGS

ASY EVENING

EASY EVENINGS

05. EASY EVENINGS 05. EASY EVENI

EASY EVENINGS

ASY EVENING

EASY EVENINGS

05. EASY EVENINGS 05. EASY EVENIN

EASY EVENINGS

EASY EVENING

Pea Pistou Soup

THE DISH

A bright green bowl of brothy, nourishing soup. Vegan pesto brings the flavour, while the texture comes from short pasta and crunchy croutons. This one is dead easy and comes together soup-er (sorry) quickly.

INGREDIENTS

1.5 litres **vegetable stock**
6 tbsp **vegan pesto**
olive oil
3 **carrots**, chopped into rough diamonds
200g **tubetti**
300g **frozen peas and broad beans**
a handful of **chunky croutons**
salt and **black pepper**

METHOD

Add the vegetable stock to a large saucepan set over a medium heat and bring to a gentle simmer. Season with salt, then add 2 tablespoons of pesto and a good glug of olive oil. Stir well.

Add the carrots to the simmering stock and cook for 2–3 minutes. Chuck in the pasta and cook for a further 8–9 minutes.

Add the frozen veggies and cook for another 2 minutes. Season to taste.

Divide between 4 warm bowls and top with the remaining pesto and a handful of croutons. Finish with a grind of black pepper before serving.

TIME: 20 MINUTES   **SERVES: 4**   **VEGAN**

6 Time-Saving Tips

There are a couple of things you always want to keep in mind for an easy midweek meal. You don't want to pull out all the stops but you don't want to compromise on flavour either. Following these tips will help you have a stress-free cooking experience, so you can spend more time eating. Which we all know is the best bit of all.

1. THINK IT THROUGH

By spending just 10 minutes reading through the recipe and gathering your ingredients beforehand, you're setting yourself up for a much speedier cooking experience. Once you've read the recipe thoroughly, you'll have an idea of what you're doing so you won't waste time constantly reading and checking. Grab any specialist equipment you'll need, too – you'll thank yourself later.

2. MINIMISE DISTRACTIONS

Turn off the podcast and put down your phone. It's so easy to get caught up in social media, conversations or something very entertaining on the TV when you're cooking but if you can enjoy the dinner-making process as a meditative experience, it'll all be over much quicker and you'll probably enjoy it a lot more, too.

3. TAKE SHORTCUTS

Make the most of what the shops have to offer. It'll cost a little bit more, but if you're strapped for time, it's more than worth it. Think rice pouches, tinned pulses and pre-chopped veggies, but also time-saving prep you can do yourself. One of our favourite shortcuts involves blitzing a bunch of garlic in a food processor, freezing that garlic paste in an ice cube tray, and then popping those garlic cubes into your recipe as you need them. No faff or having to peel garlic cloves in the heat of the moment.

4. FEEL THE HEAT

Firstly, if when you're reading through a recipe it tells you to get the oven on – do it. Making sure your oven is properly preheated will save a heap of time and means that your food cooks accurately. In the same vein, pay careful attention to how a recipe is telling you to cook something – is it supposed to be vigorously boiling but you're only on a bare simmer? This will all play into the time it takes to cook your food.

5. BATCH IT

If something you're making can be easily doubled and eaten later in the week, it's no more effort to cook more of the same dish. Bonus points if you can freeze it, too – it's meal-prepping for dummies. Even if there's just an element of the dish you can make in bulk like roasted veg, a dressing or a sauce, you'll be very grateful you took care of future-you.

6. SAVE ON WASHING UP

Wherever possible, use the packaging that food comes in to prepare it. Marinate your chicken in the container. Use the dregs of a yoghurt pot to mix the dressing in. If you're breadcrumbing something and using the last of your breadcrumbs – throw it straight into the bag to toss around. Can you boil your veggies and your couscous in the same pan? Can you wipe out the frying pan after sautéeing something and use it for the next part of the recipe? We all hate standing over the sink, so let's avoid it at all costs.

Chicken, 'Nduja + Sourdough

THE DISH

Something magic happens when the juices from the chicken saturate deep into the sourdough croutons in this dish, getting them all caramelised and intensely chicken-y. We've used a whole chicken here because it feels fancy-ish for midweek but it still cooks in the same amount of time as chicken thighs.

INGREDIENTS

1 **whole chicken** (approx. 1.5kg)
6 tbsp **'nduja**
3 tbsp **extra virgin olive oil**
5 slices of **sourdough**, roughly torn
  into chunks
300g **cherry tomatoes**
3 tbsp **crème fraîche**
5 sprigs of **basil**, leaves picked
salt and **black pepper**

METHOD

Preheat the oven to 200°C fan.

Use sharp scissors to cut down either side of the backbone (on the underside of the chicken) to remove it. Place the chicken on a baking tray. Push down on the point between the breasts until you hear a little crack to help flatten it. Pull the skin to release it from the meat slightly, then use your hand to distribute 2 tablespoons of 'nduja under the breast skin.

Season the chicken generously with salt and pepper and drizzle with olive oil. Roast for 20 minutes, then remove from the oven. Nestle the sourdough, cherry tomatoes and remaining 4 tablespoons of 'nduja around the chicken, tossing them to coat in the olive oil and juices. Return to the oven for 30 minutes. When the chicken skin is golden and crisp, and, when pierced, the juices run clear, transfer the chicken and croutons to a chopping board to rest.

Set the tray on the hob over a medium heat. Add 250ml of water to the tray and use a wooden spoon to scrape up all the tomato and 'nduja from the base. Cook for 5 minutes until the sauce has reduced slightly. Turn off the heat and stir through the crème fraîche.

Serve the chicken with the croutons and pour the sauce over everything. Garnish with basil and let everyone tuck in.

TIP

If you don't feel confident spatchcocking a chicken, watch a YouTube video or swap for 8 skin-on chicken thighs.

TIME: 1 HOUR   **SERVES: 4**   161

Harissa Sausage Orzotto

THE DISH

This is your new post-pub go-to when you want something jam-packed with flavour but don't have much to work with. Make sure you really go to town on browning the sausages – you want to get them slightly crunchy to contrast with the creamy texture of the orzo.

INGREDIENTS

4 tbsp **extra virgin olive oil**
1 **banana shallot**, diced
20g **coriander**, leaves picked, stalks
   finely chopped
4 **sausages**, meat squeezed out
2 tbsp **harissa**
100g **orzo**
60g **feta**
salt and **black pepper**

METHOD

Set a high-sided frying pan over a medium heat and add 2 tablespoons of oil, the shallot, the coriander stalks and a pinch of salt, frying gently for around 10 minutes until the shallots have softened and are translucent.

Meanwhile, set another frying pan over a medium-high heat and add 2 tablespoons of oil and the sausage meat, breaking it up into small pieces with a wooden spoon while cooking. You want the sausage to get nice and crispy for a good crunch. Once ready, mix in 1 tablespoon of harissa and set aside.

Add the orzo to the shallots and increase to a medium heat. Add 400–500ml of water gradually, stirring regularly between each addition until the water has been absorbed, which will take about 9 minutes. Once ready, mix in the remaining 1 tablespoon of harissa.

To serve, plate up the orzo, top with the sausage, then crumble over the feta. Sprinkle over the coriander leaves and finish with a grind of black pepper.

    TIME: 30 MINUTES   **SERVES: 2**

Parmesan + Pepper Risotto

THE DISH

You will not believe how creamy this cacio e pepe-style risotto gets despite having hardly any cheese in it at all. A perfect meal for the end of the month, especially when all you have are scraps and a rogue bag of risotto rice.

INGREDIENTS

1½ tbsp freshly cracked **black pepper**
50g **unsalted butter**
1 large **shallot**, finely diced
2 **garlic cloves**, finely diced or grated
120g **arborio risotto rice**
1 **stock cube** of your choice
1–2 old **Parmesan rinds**, plus a little grated Parmesan to serve
extra virgin olive oil, to drizzle
salt

METHOD

Set a deep frying pan over a medium heat and toast the freshly cracked black pepper for 1 minute until fragrant.

Add the butter and shallot and sweat for 5 minutes before adding the garlic. Fry for a further 2 minutes until fragrant.

Add the risotto rice to the pan, coating it in all the buttery goodness for 2 minutes.

Meanwhile, set a saucepan over a medium-low heat and add 1 litre of boiling water and the stock cube. Keep at a low simmer.

Gradually spoon the stock into the frying pan of risotto rice, 1 ladleful at a time, stirring very regularly. Chuck in the Parmesan rind(s) and when you can't see any liquid, continue to add more stock until the rice is tender, but slightly al dente (this may mean you don't use all of your hot stock).

Remove the Parmesan rinds before serving. Season to taste – it will likely be quite salty already from the cheese. Drizzle over a little extra virgin olive oil and a sprinkle of Parmesan to finish.

TIP

Parmesan rinds freeze really well – every time you get to the end of a wedge, pop the rind in a sandwich bag and store in the freezer until you want to make this dish, or add them to stews and ragus for an extra savoury depth.

TIME: 30 MINUTES **SERVES: 2** 165

Tikka Masala Dal

METHOD

Set a deep saucepan over a medium-low heat and add the oil, the sliced shallot and the matchstick ginger. Fry until golden and crisp, about 6 minutes, then remove from the saucepan using a slotted spoon and drain on a plate lined with kitchen paper to absorb any excess oil.

Add the finely chopped shallots to the saucepan and sauté for 5 minutes until softened and translucent. Add the grated ginger and fry for 1 minute until fragrant.

Add the tikka paste and cook for 2 minutes until the oil begins to separate and the paste reduces. Then add the red lentils and stir well to coat in the flavours.

Pour in most of the coconut milk (reserving 2 tablespoons for later) and 700ml of cold water, bring up to a boil, then reduce to a simmer for 15 minutes until the lentils have absorbed most of the liquid and are tender. Season generously with salt and pepper.

Serve with a drizzle of the reserved 2 tablespoons of coconut milk and top with the crispy shallots and ginger. Finish with an extra grind of black pepper.

THE DISH

Make yourself a batch of this warm, comforting, food-for-the-soul dal on a blustery day. It's a well-loved flavour combo, simmered with subtle spices, and cheap as chips to throw together. Check your spice paste to make sure it's vegan.

TIP

This freezes well in an airtight container for up to 3 months.

INGREDIENTS

3 tbsp **vegetable oil**
4 **shallots**, 1 sliced into rounds, 3 finely chopped
30g **fresh ginger**, peeled, ½ sliced into matchsticks, ½ finely grated
80g **tikka masala paste** (check the label if making gluten-free)
300g **red lentils**, washed and drained
1 x 400ml tin of **coconut milk**
salt and **black pepper**

Coconutty Chicken Skewers

THE DISH

This fresh and zingy main is packed with flavour and incredibly easy to make. You can enjoy it as is, or bulk it up with your carb of choice. Rice or noodles would work particularly well.

INGREDIENTS

8 **lemongrass stalks**
600ml **coconut milk**
600g skinless and boneless **chicken thighs**, sliced into strips
½ **red cabbage**, thinly sliced
75g **radishes**, thinly sliced
1 **lime**, zested and juiced, plus extra wedges to serve
salt and **black pepper**

METHOD

Bruise and roughly chop the lemongrass. Place in a blender with 400ml of the coconut milk, 2 teaspoons of salt and some black pepper and blitz.

Put the chicken thigh strips into a large bowl. Add the coconutty marinade and toss well to coat. Leave to marinate for at least 1 hour.

Meanwhile, soak 8–10 bamboo skewers in water for a minimum of 30 minutes. This will prevent them from burning under the grill.

Put the cabbage and radish slices in a large bowl, season with salt and pepper and toss to combine.

Put the lime zest (reserving some for garnish) and lime juice in a small bowl with the remaining 200ml of coconut milk, season with salt and pepper and whisk to combine.

Pour the dressing over the cabbage and radish slaw and toss to coat evenly.

Preheat the grill to medium-high. Skewer the marinated chicken and place on a baking tray under the grill for 30 minutes, turning every 10 minutes to cook evenly. Alternatively, these would be great on the BBQ.

Serve with extra lime zest and wedges.

TIME: 45 MINUTES + MARINATING   SERVES: 4   GLUTEN-FREE

Garlicky
Golden Rice

THE DISH

**This is a common dish that you might find
served in many Chinese households. The
egg yolks are what makes the rice really
rich and sticky. This dish goes great with
the braised pork belly dish on p.180.**

INGREDIENTS

200g cooked **jasmine rice**
5 **eggs**
2 tbsp **vegetable oil**
5 **garlic cloves**, 3 crushed, 2 thinly sliced
2 **spring onions**, white ends and green ends
   separated, thinly sliced
2 tbsp **Shaoxing wine** or **mirin**
100g **frozen peas**
salt and **black pepper**

METHOD

Take the rice out of the fridge and set aside.

Separate 3 eggs putting the yolks in one bowl
and their whites in another. Whisk the yolks,
then add to the cooked rice and mix well with
chopsticks or your hands so every grain of
rice is evenly coated.

Set a wok over a medium-high heat, add
1 tablespoon of oil and the egg whites.
Cook them, scrambling a little, then add the
crushed garlic and the whites of the spring
onions. Fry for just a minute.

Add the cooked rice to the wok with the
Shaoxing wine, peas and most of the green
spring onions. Season with salt and pepper.
Cook until the rice is fried and beginning to
look golden in patches. Give it a toss, then
remove from the hob.

In a separate frying pan, add a good glug of
oil over a medium heat, then add the sliced
garlic. Fry until crispy, then set aside.

Carefully separate the remaining 2 egg yolks
from the whites, keeping the yolks in their
shells. Save the whites for another recipe.

Plate up each serving with an egg yolk, some
crispy garlic and the remaining spring onions.
Finish with a grind of black pepper.

TIP

Using day-old rice is perfect as you don't have
to wait for it to cool. Microwave rice pouches
work really well too. Make sure the wok is hot
enough when you fry your rice ('wok hei') so
you get that smoky flavour.

Miso Chicory Panade

THE DISH

This savoury bread pudding is a super satisfying and warming one-pot dinner. Making great use of leftover bread, it's a casserole with big French onion soup vibes. The intensely salty and savoury miso marries well with the mild and nutty Comté.

INGREDIENTS

2 tbsp **extra virgin olive oil**
2 **leeks**, sliced
3 tbsp **white miso paste**
200g **sourdough**, torn into small chunks
3 heads of **white chicory**, quartered
200g **Comté**, grated
a small handful of **chives**, finely chopped
salt and **black pepper**

METHOD

Preheat the oven to 200°C fan.

Set a large shallow Dutch oven or casserole dish over a medium-low heat, add the olive oil and fry the leeks until slightly softened and fragrant, about 4 minutes.

Add the miso paste, sourdough and chicory and stir to coat everything.

Add two-thirds of the Comté and stir, then season to taste. Pour over 400ml of water and turn off the heat.

Sprinkle the remaining Comté on top and bake for 30 minutes until the exposed parts of the sourdough turn golden and crisp and most of the liquid has been absorbed.

Allow to sit for 5 minutes, then sprinkle over the chives to serve.

SWAP

If you can't find Comté, Gruyère or Cheddar make wonderful swaps.

TIME: 45 MINUTES   **SERVES: 4**   **VEGGIE   173**

'Nduja Cod with Butter Bean Mash

METHOD

Set a saucepan over a medium heat with 2 tablespoons of olive oil. Add the garlic and fry for a minute until fragrant. Do not let it brown, as this will make your beans bitter.

Tip the butter beans into the pan (liquid and all), then fill a quarter of the empty jar with water and add this to the pan too. Simmer for 10 minutes, then lightly mash the beans. You want some to stay whole, and some to form a delicious creamy mush. Season to taste, then set aside and keep warm.

Set a frying pan over a medium heat and melt 100g of butter, then spoon in the 'nduja, letting it melt down for a couple of minutes until the butter turns a nice bright red.

Set a large non-stick frying pan over a medium-high heat with 1 tablespoon of olive oil. Season the cod fillets with salt, then add them to the pan, skin-side down. Fry for 3 minutes until the skin is nice and crispy, and most of the flesh on the skin side has turned opaque, then flip the fillet over. If the cod fillets are thick, cook for 1–2 minutes on the other side, otherwise turn off the heat and allow the residual heat to finish the cooking.

Add the remaining 25g of butter to the frying pan. Once it has melted, use a spoon to baste the fish with it. The fish is cooked when the flesh has turned opaque and flaky.

To serve, spoon the butter bean mash onto plates, then top each with a fillet of fish. Spoon over the 'nduja butter and serve with a wedge of lemon on the side.

THE DISH

A very classy dish indeed. The spicy fattiness of 'nduja is the perfect thing to drench a flaky piece of cod. We recommend using a nice jar of butter beans, but tinned would work, too.

INGREDIENTS

3 tbsp **olive oil**
2 **garlic cloves**, finely chopped
1 x 600g jar of **butter beans**
125g **salted butter**
60g **'nduja**
4 skin-on **cod fillets**
1 **lemon**, cut into wedges
salt and **black pepper**

TIME: 20 MINUTES   **SERVES: 4**   **GLUTEN-FREE**

Burrata, Cornichon + Potato Bake

THE DISH

We still can't quite believe that this recipe contains just 6 ingredients. It's got everything you'd ever want in a meal – crispy potatoes, prosciutto, a sharp green dressing and a sexy ball of burrata on top. Not only that, but all you need is one dish to bring it all together. Winner.

INGREDIENTS

500g **baby potatoes**
7 tbsp **olive oil**
2 heads of **red chicory**, quartered
80g slices of **prosciutto**
a large handful of **tarragon**, finely chopped
60g **jarred cornichons**, finely chopped, plus
    1 tbsp pickling liquid
1 ball of **burrata**
salt and **black pepper**

METHOD

Preheat the oven to 220°C fan.

Add the potatoes to a large baking tray and drizzle with 3 tablespoons of olive oil and a generous sprinkle of salt. Roast for 40 minutes.

Remove the potatoes from the oven, then nestle in the chicory quarters and prosciutto slices. Return to the oven for 10 minutes.

Meanwhile, mix the tarragon and cornichons in a bowl with 4 tablespoons of olive oil and the cornichon pickling liquid. Stir to combine and season to taste with salt and pepper.

When the potatoes and prosciutto are crispy, and the chicory is soft, remove the tray from the oven. Tear over the burrata, then drizzle over the cornichon salsa and add a grind of black pepper to serve.

TIP

If there are any little pickled onions in your cornichon jar, chop up a few of them and chuck them in your dressing.

TIME: 1 HOUR   SERVES: 2   GLUTEN-FREE   177

Tzatziki, Lamb + Smashed Potatoes

Preheat the oven to 190°C fan.

Add the potatoes to a large saucepan of cold salted water, then set over a medium heat and bring up to a boil. Cook for 10–12 minutes until very tender when pierced with a fork. Drain, then transfer to a large baking tray. Use the bottom of a pan or a heavy glass to press firmly down on the centre of each potato until it smashes, but stays in one craggy piece. Drizzle all the potatoes with 3 tablespoons of olive oil and season with salt and pepper. Roast for 30–35 minutes until golden and crisp.

Meanwhile, season the lamb chops with salt, squeeze over ½ a lemon and set aside.

After 15 minutes, set a large frying pan over a low heat and add the lamb chops, fat-side down, to begin rendering the fat strip that is typically present. After 5 minutes, there should be visible liquid fat in the pan and the fat strip should be starting to go brown. At this point, increase the heat and cook the chops for 2 minutes on each side to get pink lamb chops with a deeply golden exterior. Set aside to rest.

While the potatoes finish cooking and the lamb chops rest, pop the cherry tomatoes in a bowl, squeeze over another lemon half and season generously with salt and pepper. Sprinkle over half of the dill and toss with the remaining 2 tablespoons of olive oil.

Serve the lamb chops on a bed of tzatziki with the crispy potatoes, marinated tomato salad and lemon wedges, with the remaining dill leaves to garnish.

THE DISH

Crisp yet tender lamb chops on cooling tzatziki with an unassuming but super tasty tomato salsa. Every element of this riffable midweek dinner will make you feel like you're on a summer holiday.

INGREDIENTS

500g **baby potatoes**
5 tbsp **extra virgin olive oil**
4 **lamb chops** or 8 **lamb cutlets**
2 **lemons**, 1 halved, 1 cut into wedges
150g **cherry tomatoes**, halved
a large handful of **dill** leaves, roughly chopped
4 tbsp **tzatziki**
salt and **black pepper**

TIME: 1 HOUR   SERVES: 2   GLUTEN-FREE

Sweet Soy-Braised Pork Belly

THE DISH

Braised pork belly doesn't have to be complicated to be delicious, and this simple recipe is proof of just that. The pork belly is full of flavour, super glossy and, honestly, pretty damn addictive. Let it bubble away on the hob while you unwind from a day's work and serve it with a bowl of fluffy rice.

INGREDIENTS

500g **pork belly**, sliced into 3cm chunks
2 tbsp **vegetable oil**
1½ tbsp **ginger garlic paste**
4 tbsp **caster sugar**
4 tbsp **dark soy sauce**
240g **white rice**
2 **spring onions**, thinly sliced
salt and **black pepper**

METHOD

Set a large saucepan of water over a medium heat and bring to a boil. Blanch the pork belly for 2 minutes, then plunge into a large bowl of icy cold water to stop the cooking.

Set a wok over a high heat and add the oil. Fry the pork belly until golden. Add the ginger garlic paste and fry until fragrant. Add the sugar and allow it to melt and bubble up.

Add the soy sauce and season well, then pour in enough water to cover the pork. When the water starts to boil, reduce the heat and let it all braise for an hour.

Wash the rice in a saucepan and give it a good rinse until the water runs clear. Then fill the saucepan with water until it reaches your first knuckle when the tip of your finger touches the rice. Set over a high heat and bring to a boil for 2 minutes. Once it's started to boil, lower the heat, pop a lid on and simmer for 12 minutes. Turn off the heat and leave the rice to cool to room temperature.

By now the pork should be nice and tender, and the water should have evaporated away, leaving a sauce that has reduced to a sticky coating.

Serve the braised pork belly with a scattering of spring onions and fluffy rice.

TIME: 1 HOUR 20 MINUTES   SERVES: 4   GLUTEN-FREE

impressive
impressive
impressive
impressive
impressive
impressive

impressive impressive impressive
impressive impressive impressive
impressive impressive impressive
impressive impressive impressive
impressive impressive impressive
impressive impressive impressive

Chipotle Chicken + Pineapple Tacos

THE DISH

You don't need an ingredients list as long as your forearm to make some ace tacos. Baking the chicken on top of the onions is the move here – it gets those onions all jammy and lovely from the chicken juices. Whatever you do, do not let that chicken skin go to waste. The texture of a crispy chicken skin wafer is an absolute hit.

INGREDIENTS

8 skin-on, bone-in **chicken thighs**,
　skins removed
3 tbsp **chipotle paste**
8 tbsp **olive oil**
3 **red onions**, 2 finely sliced, 1 finely diced
1 small **pineapple**, peeled and sliced into
　1cm-thick rounds
a large handful of **coriander** leaves,
　roughly chopped
8 **corn tortillas**
salt

METHOD

Preheat the oven to 220°C fan. Lay the chicken skins flat on a large baking tray lined with baking paper. Cover with another sheet of baking paper and set aside.

In a small bowl, mix the chipotle paste with 5 tablespoons of oil and a generous pinch of salt. Rub this all over the chicken thighs.

Add the sliced onions to another large baking tray and drizzle with olive oil and salt. Place the chicken thighs on top. Nestle this tray on top of the chicken skin tray, then roast for 40 minutes. After 20 minutes, the skin should be almost crisp – at this point, separate the 2 trays, remove the baking paper covering the skin and return the trays to the oven. Remove the chicken skin tray after 5 minutes, season well with salt and allow to cool.

Meanwhile, set a griddle pan over a high heat. Brush the pineapple slices with olive oil, then place in the pan a few at a time. Griddle for a few minutes on each side to get deep char lines. Once the pineapple is cool enough to handle, finely dice the slices. In a bowl, mix the diced red onion and pineapple with a pinch of salt, then leave to marinate and pickle slightly. When it has pickled slightly, stir most of the coriander through it.

When cooked, remove the chicken tray from the oven. Shred up the chicken with 2 forks, discarding the bones. Mix it up so the onions, chicken and chipotle sauce are all combined.

Heat the corn tortillas directly over a flame, or in a dry frying pan over a medium heat. To serve, spoon the chicken into the tacos, add some salsa, then top with the crispy chicken skin and any remaining coriander.

TIME: 1 HOUR　　　　**SERVES: 4**

Red Pepper Scallops Pil Pil

THE DISH

This is amazing as an impressive starter or as part of a Spanish-style spread. We took our inspiration from the ubiquitous Gambas Pil Pil but switched it up by using scallops instead – the citrussy roasted red peppers make a wonderful, highly spoonable sauce. You can use prawns, or any other protein if you like, but don't be scared to try it out with scallops. They're speedy to cook and are so mild, tender and sweet you'll be wondering why you don't eat 'em more often.

INGREDIENTS

1 x 450g jar of **roasted red peppers**, drained
90ml **extra virgin olive oil**
16 **scallops**
5 **garlic cloves**, thinly sliced
1 tsp **smoked paprika**
250g **asparagus**, halved if thick
1 **lemon**, halved
salt and **black pepper**

METHOD

Use a food processor or stick blender to blitz the peppers, keeping it a little chunky. Set a saucepan over a medium heat and add the blitzed peppers along with 2 tablespoons of olive oil. Season generously and cook for 10 minutes until reduced and thickened.

Pat the scallops dry with kitchen paper – if your scallops are from the fishmonger, you may have to remove a membrane or waste tract – watch a video on YouTube to see how.

Preheat a large frying pan and season the scallops on both sides with salt. Add 1 tablespoon of olive oil to the pan, then fry for 1–2 minutes on each side over a medium heat until you have a good sear on each flat surface of the scallop. It can help to push down with your spatula to get as much contact as possible with the pan. Remove the scallops from the pan and place on a baking tray to rest.

Add the remaining oil to the scallops pan with the garlic and paprika and fry for 2 minutes until vivid red and fragrant.

Set another frying pan over a high heat, then griddle the asparagus for 2–3 minutes until tender and slightly charred.

Spread the red pepper sauce on the base of a platter. Scatter over the asparagus and top with the scallops, drizzling all of that red garlicky oil over the top. Season again and serve with 2 lemon halves, squeezing generously over the platter before eating.

Ras El Hanout Lamb Shoulder

THE DISH

We can't even begin to describe the smell that will be wafting from your kitchen when you've got this in the oven. The onions and apricots soak up all that wonderful roasting liquid and become the softest, sweetest little side dish. The cook time will vary depending on the size of your lamb. Serve with a whole pomegranate cut into sections for a show-stopping garnish.

INGREDIENTS

1 **whole shoulder of lamb**, on the bone
7 tbsp **extra virgin olive oil**
2 tbsp **ras el hanout**
5 **onions**, 4 thickly sliced into rounds,
   1 finely sliced
90g **dried apricots**
240g **couscous**
200g **pomegranate seeds**
salt and **black pepper**

METHOD

With a sharp knife, stud the lamb all over. Mix 4 tablespoons of oil and the ras el hanout and rub over the lamb. Season generously with salt and pepper. Cover and marinate for at least 1 hour (out of the fridge) or up to 24 hours if you have time, storing it in the fridge until 1 hour before going into the oven. Preheat the oven to 200°C fan.

Add the thickly sliced onions to a deep baking tray in a single layer and put the lamb on top. Add 500ml of water to the bottom of the tray, being careful to avoid the lamb. Cook for 30 minutes, then lower to 130°C fan for 2 hours.

Remove from the oven and place the apricots beneath the lamb. If you notice the lamb is taking on too much colour, cover it with foil. Cook for another hour, by which time the lamb should be tender and falling off the bone – if not, continue to check on it in 15-minute increments. Remove the lamb from the oven and set aside to rest for 20–30 minutes.

Place the couscous in a heatproof bowl and pour boiling water over, until it comes just above the couscous. Cover with cling film or a lid that fits and leave to stand for 10 minutes.

Meanwhile, set a frying pan over a high heat and pour in the remaining 3 tablespoons of oil. Add the finely sliced onions and fry until crispy. Transfer to a plate lined with kitchen paper to drain any excess oil.

Fluff the couscous with a fork, season and stir through most of the pomegranate seeds. On a platter, serve the lamb over the couscous with the onions and apricots. Sprinkle over the crispy onions and remaining pomegranate seeds. Serve with a jug of the roasting juices.

Miso Mussels with Charred Corn

THE DISH

Don't be shy with the Thai basil as a good whack of the stuff injects some fragrance and complexity into the broth. Go to town on the corn, too – you want it to be thoroughly charred. Don't forget to serve this one with napkins, it can get messy!

INGREDIENTS

2 **corn on the cob**
2 tbsp **olive oil**, plus extra to drizzle
2½ tbsp **white miso paste**
a large bunch of **Thai basil**, stalks and
    leaves separated
300ml **white wine**
300ml **double cream**
2kg **mussels**, cleaned (see Tip)
salt

METHOD

Peel the husks off the corn, if they have them, and wash the cobs. Set a large saucepan of salted water over a medium heat and bring to a boil. Add the corn and cook for 6 minutes until just tender. Char over a BBQ, gas hob or under a hot grill.

When cool enough to handle, stand the corn in a bowl and cut off the kernels. Set aside.

Set a large, high-sided saucepan over a high heat. Add 2 tablespoons of oil and then add the miso and basil stalks. Fry, stirring constantly, for 2–3 minutes until toasted and the miso is starting to caramelise and catch on the saucepan.

With the heat still high, add the white wine to deglaze the saucepan. Bring to a simmer and add the cream. Bring back up to a simmer.

Add the mussels and the corn kernels, toss in the sauce, bring to a boil and pop on a lid. Cook for 5–6 minutes. Remove the lid, throw in the basil leaves and stir them through the mussels, corn and sauce.

Finish with a generous drizzle of olive oil and serve family-style in the middle of the table.

TIP

To 'clean' your mussels, give them a good scrub under running water, pulling out any long hairy bits. Only cook mussels that are closed – if any are open, give them a tap on the side of the sink and if they don't contract and close, discard them. Once cooked, only consume mussels that have opened.

TIME: 40 MINUTES   **SERVES: 4**   **GLUTEN-FREE**   191

Sesame Crackling Pulled Mushroom Buns

THE DISH

All the vibes of a hog roast, with none of the hog. There's some serious culinary alchemy that takes place when you roast sesame seeds and grind them up with a pinch of smoked paprika and flaky sea salt – it tastes just like crackling. Seriously. This recipe makes extra sesame crackling, so sprinkle it on anything for a porky fix.

INGREDIENTS

1kg **oyster mushrooms**
500g **onions**, finely sliced
100ml **olive oil**
2 tsp **smoked paprika**
30g **sesame seeds**
6 **burger buns**
300g **ready-made apple sauce**
flaky salt and **black pepper**

METHOD

Preheat the oven to 180°C fan. Add the mushrooms and onions to a deep baking tray with the olive oil and 1½ teaspoons of smoked paprika. Season very well, then pour in 100ml of water and roast for 1½ hours, stirring once or twice until the mushrooms and onions are roasted and caramelised.

Meanwhile, set a small, dry frying pan over a medium heat and add the sesame seeds. Roast until deeply golden and fragrant – they need to turn dark to get flavour. Pour straight into a pestle and mortar, then bash until they have a sand-like consistency – alternatively, you could blitz them in a food processor. Mix in the remaining smoked paprika and a teaspoon of flaky salt. Voilà, that's the sesame crackling.

Remove the mushroom and onion baking tray from the oven, shred with 2 forks to resemble pulled pork and toss through the cooking juices.

Heat the grill to its highest setting. Lay the burger buns open, face-up on a large baking tray, and grill for 1 minute until toasted.

Pour the apple sauce into a small saucepan and set over a low heat until warm.

To serve, spread some apple sauce on the bottom of each bun, pile the mushroom and onion mixture on top, sprinkle with sesame crackling and finish with the bun lids.

SWAP

This works well with king oyster mushrooms, too, but it's best to shred them before roasting.

TIME: 1 HOUR 45 MINUTES   SERVES: 6   VEGAN

Proper Garlic Roast Chicken

METHOD

Sprinkle salt and black pepper all over the chicken and set aside in a small baking tray. It helps to do this a few hours, or up to a day ahead, to tenderise the meat, or you can crack on straight away.

Preheat the oven to 190°C fan.

Remove the leaves from some of the thyme sprigs and sprinkle over the chicken. Stuff most of the remaining bunch into the cavity of the chicken, setting aside some thyme for garnish later. Nestle the whole garlic bulbs around the chicken in the baking tray.

If the potato halves seem too big, cut the potatoes into thirds and add to a large saucepan of salted cold water.

Set the pan over a medium-high heat and bring to a boil, cooking the potatoes for 10 minutes, or until easily pierced with a knife. Drain the potatoes and shake them around in the colander until fluffy – don't worry if some break apart, this just creates more delicious crunchy bits. Allow to steam dry in the sink for 5–10 minutes.

Meanwhile, pop the chicken into the oven on the top shelf. Set a timer for 50 minutes. Then, pour enough olive oil into a large baking tray to coat the bottom, and place in the oven on the bottom shelf for 5–10 minutes to heat up.

Once the oil is hot, pour the potatoes onto the tray and use 2 spoons to coat the potatoes on all sides with the oil. Season with salt and return to the oven to roast for 25 minutes.

THE DISH

Not gonna lie, we're pretty impressed that we've been able to make such a belter of a roast dinner with so few ingredients. It might feel excessive to roast this much garlic, but it makes the whole gravy sing.

INGREDIENTS

1 **whole chicken** (approx. 1.5kg)
a bunch of **thyme** sprigs
4 **garlic bulbs**
800g **Maris Piper potatoes**, peeled and halved
olive oil
500g **carrots**, cut into batons
1 **savoy cabbage**, cut into wedges
salt and **black pepper**

TIME: 1 HOUR 45 MINUTES   **SERVES: 4**   **GLUTEN-FREE**   195

METHOD CONTINUED

After 25 minutes, remove the tray of potatoes from the oven, nestle the carrots in among the potatoes and return to the oven for a further 30 minutes.

When your 50-minute timer goes off, check the chicken is cooked through by poking a small, sharp knife into the deepest section of the thigh, leave it inside for 10 seconds, then immediately test the temperature of the knife on the inside of your wrist. If it instantly feels very hot and, when pierced between the thigh and the breast, the juices run clear, your chicken is cooked. If it's just warm, it probably needs 5–10 minutes more. Remove the chicken from the oven and set aside to rest in its tray.

Remove the potato and carrot tray from the oven and nestle in the cabbage wedges, drizzling it with a bit of olive oil and seasoning with salt and pepper. Return to the oven for 15–20 minutes until the potatoes are golden and crisp, the carrots are tender and the cabbage is beginning to catch.

Now to make a gravy – remove the chicken from the baking tray, making sure to tip it, cavity-side down, to allow all of the juice from inside the chicken to pour into the tray. Pop it on a chopping board to carve later.

Use a knife to chop off the tip of each garlic bulb, then squeeze the soft garlic directly into the tray, mashing it roughly with a wooden spoon and discarding the papery skins.

Turn on the hob underneath the baking tray and use a wooden spoon to scrape up any caramelised bits off the base. Add 250–300ml of water and stir well. Let it come up to a boil and keep stirring until you have a gravy-ish consistency. Pour the gravy into a warmed jug and set aside.

Carve the chicken, pouring any more juices that have seeped out into the gravy, then serve with the potatoes, carrots and cabbage, and garnish with some fresh thyme leaves.

Ribeye with Curry Butter Hash Browns

THE DISH

Can you wow a crowd of hungry diners with just 6 ingredients? Yes. Yes, you can. And all you have to do is make this big, meaty centrepiece. The giant, crispy, caramelised hash browns smothered in curry butter almost steal the show. But we guess the steak is pretty good, too.

INGREDIENTS

200g **unsalted butter**, softened
2 tbsp **madras curry paste** (check the label if making gluten-free)
4 **limes**
4 **red onions**, thinly sliced
900g–1kg bone-in **ribeye steak**
2kg **Maris Piper potatoes**, peeled and coarsely grated
5–6 tbsp **olive oil**
salt and **black pepper**

METHOD

Preheat the oven to 150°C fan.

Add the butter to a food processor along with the curry paste and the zest and juice of 2 limes. Blitz together and season with salt. Set aside.

Toss a quarter of the sliced red onions with a handful of salt and the juice of 1 lime in a bowl. Set aside to quickly pickle.

Season the ribeye generously with salt, and really go to town here, it's a big piece of meat and we want every bite to be seasoned beautifully. Set aside.

When you grate the potatoes, use a food processor with a grater attachment if you've got one, but a box grater will work just fine! Try to make the strands as long as you can.

Rinse the potato gratings 3 or 4 times in cold water to remove excess starch. Dry thoroughly with a salad spinner or clean tea towels, squeezing well to remove as much liquid as you can.

Set a large, non-stick frying pan over a medium heat and add half of the olive oil. Add half of the potatoes in an even layer and press down so it fills the pan to the edges, making a large circular hash brown, and season thoroughly.

Cook for 10–15 minutes until brown and crisp, flip out onto a plate, then return to the pan, raw-side down. Cook for another 10 minutes until fully crisp and cooked through. Transfer to a baking tray and repeat with the remaining potato mixture and oil to make a second hash brown.

Meanwhile, set a cast iron skillet or heavy frying pan over a medium-high heat. You don't want it raging hot; it's a big piece of meat and if you start too strong it'll be burnt by the time it's cooked.

Colour the steak all over, starting by rendering the fat and creating a good crust. This should take roughly 8–9 minutes.

Add 2 tablespoons of the curry butter to the pan and baste the steak briefly once it has melted. Transfer the steak to a baking tray and pour over the hot butter from the pan. Transfer to the oven for 7–8 minutes. If you have a meat thermometer, you're looking for 47°C for a perfect medium–rare.

Remove the steak from the oven and rest for 10 minutes. Meanwhile, return the steak pan to a high heat and add the rest of the onions. Cook with a big pinch of salt for 9–10 minutes until caramelised and jammy.

Brush the hash browns with curry butter and cut each into 6 portions. Carve the steak from the bone and cut into 2cm-thick slices. Serve with melted curry butter, lime wedges and the pickled and jammy onions.

Serve the lot family-style at the table and get stuck in.

6 Tips for Having People Over

1. DO YOUR HOMEWORK

Firstly, you want to think long and hard about your invite list. Try and aim for a mix of people who already know each other and a few who don't, but you just know will hit it off. You want to make sure the conversation can flow without you when you're busy being the perfect host and putting all the finishing touches to the meal. Absolutely do not, under any circumstances, forget to ask about dietary requirements before the night. There's nothing worse than making a big meat feast and then finding out one of your guests has recently become a vegan.

2. LIGHTING IS EVERYTHING

You don't have to rewire your flat but think about lighting that's cosy, informal and above all else, flattering. That means candles – as many as you can possibly find. Try popping down to your local charity shop where you're always guaranteed to find a surplus of cute, mismatched candle holders. Failing that, just stick a bunch of tea lights on the table. Be careful not to set yourselves on fire, of course. And, for goodness' sake, turn off the big light – we want low lamps in the room only, please.

3. SETTING THE TABLE

Ideally, you want this to be done before anyone arrives. There's no need for anything as formal as place names, but it's good to have an idea about where you might want people to sit and make sure you bagsy the seat closest to the kitchen so you're not squeezing yourself in after serving up. It's the little details like water on the table, cute napkins and even a few simple supermarket flowers that will really take the experience to the next level.

4. BE PREPARED

That means reading through the recipe before you start and doing any and all prep you can before your guests show up. Even if you're reheating something when they arrive, that's better than you being absent from your friends for an hour because you underestimated how long it was going to take to roast a chicken. Trust me: we're speaking from personal experience here. If people arrive early, don't feel bad about putting them to work. Most guests love being helpful, so get them to pick herbs or plate up nibbles so you can focus on the rest of the meal.

5. CHOOSE THE RIGHT MUSIC

Don't neglect the tunes. Make sure you've got a lengthy playlist (at least 3 hours) but don't turn it up too high. You want to inspire conversation, not have people shouting over each other and Mazzy Star. Sometimes it's fun to be thematic with the music – try out the Chef soundtrack for a taco night or go for some chilled Parisian vibes when you're making coq au vin. If you're ever in a pinch, we have a bunch of playlists for you to choose from on our Spotify page.

6. DON'T APOLOGISE

When you sit down, don't you dare even think about apologising. Sure, you might not have got all the ingredients, you might have left the dish in the oven for 20 minutes too long, or you might even have swapped the salt for sugar but there's nothing worse than an insecure host. No one wants to hear a play-by-play of the recipe and its trials and tribulations – they're hungry! And they love you. Serve it. They'll enjoy it. Laugh about it afterwards, if necessary.

Chicken Parm
Garlic Flatbreads

METHOD

Preheat the oven to 180°C fan.

Set a medium frying pan over a medium heat. Add the olive oil, chopped tomatoes and a few basil leaves and season generously with salt and pepper. Simmer for 20 minutes until the sauce is reduced. Set aside and keep warm.

Meanwhile, salt the chicken breasts and lay between 2 sheets of baking paper. Use the bottom of a heavy saucepan or a rolling pin to flatten out the chicken breasts until they are an even thickness, around 1½cm. Set aside.

Pop the flatbreads on baking trays and cook for 8–10 minutes until golden. Allow to cool slightly, then blitz 2 into crumbs using a food processor. Pile the crumbs onto a large plate.

Add the mayonnaise to a shallow bowl and dunk the chicken breasts. Use a spoon to coat them fully and to remove any excess – you want a thin film of mayo on each. Toss the chicken in the breadcrumbs and coat evenly, using your hands to press the crumbs onto the chicken.

Pour oil into a large frying pan to coat the bottom to a 1cm depth. Set over a medium heat and, when the oil starts to shimmer, fry the chicken in batches until golden on each side (it will get baked in the oven, so don't worry about cooking through). Take straight from the pan to a baking tray, and bake for 5–7 minutes until cooked through.

To assemble, slice the 4 remaining flatbreads in 2 and spread half of them with mayo. Lay a chicken fillet on top, then 2–3 tablespoons of tomato sauce, a handful of Parmesan, a grind of black pepper and 3–4 basil leaves. Top with a flatbread slice to serve.

THE DISH

Coating the chicken in mayonnaise before the breadcrumbs is a total game-changer – it's one of those hacks you'll be telling everyone about, regardless of whether or not they care how you bread your chicken.

INGREDIENTS

2 tbsp **extra virgin olive oil**
2 x 400g tins of **finely chopped tomatoes**
a bunch of **basil** leaves
4 **chicken breast fillets**
6 **garlic flatbreads** (approx. 190g each)
60g **mayonnaise**, plus extra to spread
vegetable oil, to fry
50g **Parmesan**, grated
salt and **black pepper**

TIME: 50 MINUTES   **SERVES: 4**   203

Kimchi Ketjap Salmon Traybake

Impressive

THE DISH

Sticky, funky and sharp – this is one of those quick-fix dinners to always keep in your back pocket for an emergency dinner party. A side of salmon cooks in 15 minutes or less, so you can spend more time chatting and less time faffing.

INGREDIENTS

300g **kimchi**
3 tbsp **ketjap manis** or **dark soy sauce**
   (check the label if making gluten-free)
1 **side of salmon** (approx. 800g–1kg)
8 **spring onions**, 7 whole, 1 thinly sliced
350g **Tenderstem broccoli**, woody ends
   removed
3 tbsp **vegetable oil**
2 tbsp **sesame seeds** (we used black and white)

METHOD

Preheat the oven to 190°C fan.

Put half of the kimchi and 2 tablespoons of ketjap manis into a food processor and blitz – this is the marinade.

Lay the side of salmon down the middle of a large baking tray. Cover with the marinade. Nestle the whole spring onions and broccoli around the salmon so they are evenly distributed – you may need to use 2 trays as we don't want the veg to steam.

Drizzle the oil over the salmon and veggies, then sprinkle over the sesame seeds and roast for 12–15 minutes until the salmon is coral-coloured inside and the vegetables are beginning to char.

Remove from the oven and drizzle the remaining ketjap manis over the veg. Scatter the remaining kimchi over the salmon and serve garnished with the sliced spring onion.

SWAP

Ketjap manis is a sticky, sweet soy sauce often used in Indonesian cookery – it makes a delicious savoury marinade here, but you can swap it with dark soy sauce if you can't find it in your supermarket.

TIME: 25 MINUTES   **SERVES: 4**   **GLUTEN-FREE**   205

Cumin Carrot Tarte Tatin

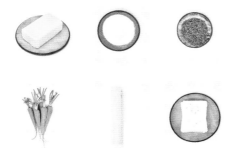

THE DISH

Tarte tatin isn't just for pudding. Sticky cumin-spiced carrots take the place of traditional apples here, while crumbling feta over the top is what gives it a zippy, savoury edge. If you can get carrots with their tops still on, those can make a lovely green garnish. Don't sweat it if not.

INGREDIENTS

60g **salted butter**
60g **caster sugar**
1 tbsp **cumin seeds**
200g **baby carrots with tops**, halved
1 sheet of **ready-rolled puff pastry**
100g **feta**
sea salt

You will need a 25cm ovenproof frying pan.

METHOD

Preheat the oven to 190°C fan.

Set a 25cm ovenproof frying pan over a medium heat, then add the butter to melt.

Reduce the heat to low, sprinkle in the sugar and cumin seeds, swirling around to melt the sugar. Allow to cook until the sugar has bubbled away and has turned a light, toffee colour. Add a big pinch of sea salt.

Arrange the carrots tidily in the pan, cut-side down, slicing a couple in half so that they can fit around the edges. Once the first layer is covered, slot in any remaining carrots on top. Pour in 50ml of water and gently simmer for 5 minutes to lightly cook the carrots.

Meanwhile, roll out the puff pastry sheet and cut out a circle the size of your frying pan, then prick all over with a fork. Place the pastry circle on top of the carrots, tucking in the edges, being careful not to burn your fingers. It can help to use a knife. Pop the frying pan in the oven for 30 minutes.

When fully cooked and the pastry is golden, remove from the oven, place a large plate on top and carefully flip the pan over to release the tart. If the carrots don't look golden and sticky enough, place on a baking tray and cook for a further 5–10 minutes. Crumble over the feta and garnish with the carrot tops, if using, before serving. Finish with a grind of black pepper.

TIP

Make cheese twists or puff pastry croutons with any excess puff pastry.

TIME: 50 MINUTES   **SERVES: 4**   **VEGGIE**

Manchego + Romesco Celeriac Steaks

THE DISH

Although impressive, this veg-packed meal is easy enough to become a Tuesday-night-and-you're-knackered staple. Romesco sauce normally contains a few more ingredients, but we've distilled it down to its key components: toasted almonds, roasted peppers and smoked paprika. Keep it simple.

INGREDIENTS

1 large **celeriac**, peeled and sliced into
   2½cm-thick discs
olive oil
2 tbsp **sweet smoked paprika**
50g **flaked almonds**
1 x 450g jar of **roasted red peppers**, drained
125g **Manchego**, grated
300g **Tenderstem broccoli**, woody ends
   removed
salt

METHOD

Preheat the oven to 210°C fan.

Rub the celeriac steaks with olive oil, 1 tablespoon of smoked paprika and some salt.

Set a frying pan over a medium heat. Add the celeriac discs and fry for about 4 minutes on each side until golden and just starting to soften. Remove from the pan and set aside. This will likely need to be done in batches.

Place the fried celeriac steaks on a baking tray, then put in the oven for 15 minutes.

Meanwhile, add the flaked almonds to the frying pan that you used for the celeriac and toast over a medium heat for 5 minutes until golden.

Tip most of the almonds into a food processor, reserving a handful for later. Rinse the peppers, then pop these in too, along with 1 tablespoon of smoked paprika, and blitz.

Remove the tray from the oven, flip the celeriac steaks and add 2 tablespoons of the red sauce on top, then sprinkle with the Manchego. Nestle the broccoli around the celeriac and drizzle with a little olive oil and salt. Return to the oven for another 15 minutes until the cheese has melted and the broccoli is tender and beginning to catch.

Scatter with the remaining almonds, then serve with some extra sauce.

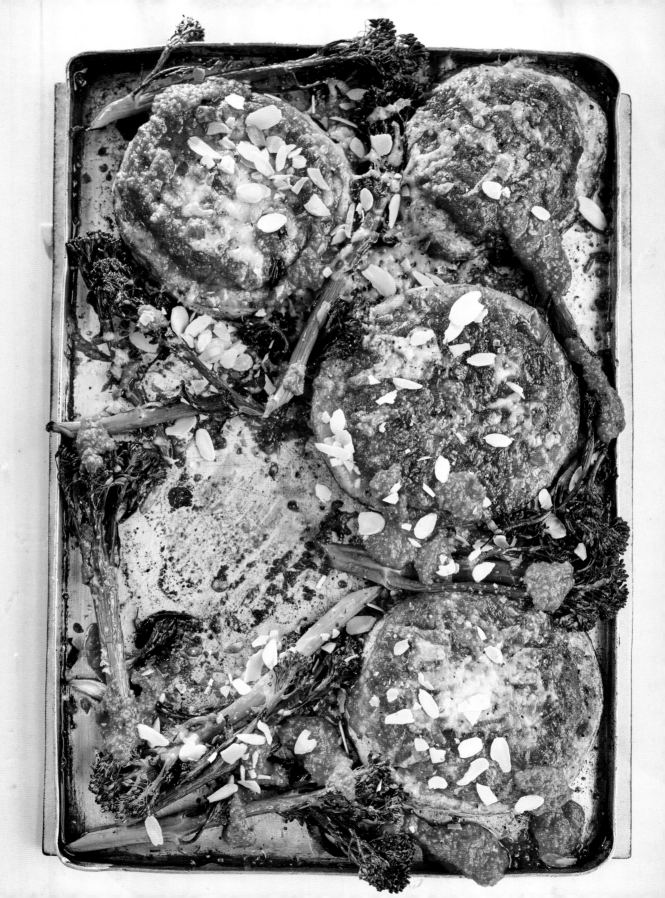

Mackerel with Squashed Tomatoes

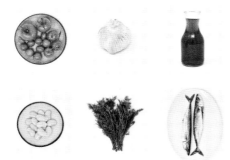

THE DISH

Mackerel is super affordable, super tasty and dead simple to cook. This is a great late-summer Sunday lunch. You can make the salad a few hours in advance as the longer it sits, the better it gets. Try to get your hands on really, really good jarred beans for maximum flavour and texture.

INGREDIENTS

1kg **mixed heritage tomatoes**, sliced into irregular chunks
1 **garlic bulb**, cloves peeled
250ml **olive oil**
3 tbsp **sherry vinegar**, plus extra if needed
2 x 600g jars of **butter beans**, drained and rinsed
a large handful of **dill** leaves, roughly chopped
2 large or 4 small **filleted whole mackerel**
salt and **black pepper**

METHOD

Put the tomato chunks in a large bowl, season generously with salt and scrunch with your hands to squash the tomatoes slightly. Set aside.

Place the garlic in a small saucepan and cover with the oil. Set over a low heat and cook for 5–10 minutes until the garlic has softened. Set aside to cool in the oil.

Drain 3–4 tablespoons of the tomato-ey water from the bowl of tomatoes and pour into a jar. Add the sherry vinegar and a big pinch of salt and pepper. Pour 85ml of the confit garlic oil into the jar, put on a lid and shake to create a dressing. Tip away the rest of the water from the tomato bowl – you can always save this or drink it!

Remove the garlic from the oil and toss into the bowl of tomatoes, setting the oil aside. Add the butter beans along with most of the dill. Add the dressing, toss, taste and season with extra vinegar and salt if it needs it.

Preheat the grill to high. Rub the mackerel fillets in a little of the garlic oil and season generously with salt. Place on a baking tray and slide under the grill for 4–6 minutes, flipping halfway, until the skin is crisp and the flesh is white, cooked through and flaking away.

Serve the fish on top of the tomato salad, scattered with the remaining dill.

TIME: 30 MINUTES   **SERVES: 4**   **GLUTEN-FREE**   211

Chickpea Gnocchi, Broad Beans + Lemon

THE DISH

You might know this delightfully delicate and crisp gnocchi as panisse or panelle – a chickpea-based fritter or chip from France and Sicily, respectively. We've reimagined it as gnocchi and it's bloody perfect. A crisp exterior and delightfully custardy interior make this the best damn gnocchi you've ever had.

INGREDIENTS

280g **salted butter**
200g **chickpea (gram) flour**
4 tbsp **olive oil**, plus extra for greasing
250g **fresh broad beans**, podded
1 **lemon**, zested and juiced
Parmesan, grated, to serve
a large handful of **basil** leaves
salt and **black pepper**

You will need a 20x20cm brownie tin.

METHOD

Put 180g of the butter in a saucepan with 500ml of cold water. Set over a medium heat and bring up to a boil.

Meanwhile, add the chickpea flour to a bowl and slowly pour in 200ml of water, whisking well to make a lump-free batter.

Grease a 20x20cm brownie tin with a little oil and set aside.

Once the butter and water mixture is boiling, pour in the chickpea flour mixture and cook over a low heat, whisking continuously for 8–10 minutes until it has substantially thickened and a dry film is coating the base of the pan. It should be the texture of a thick smooth cake batter or loose mashed potatoes. Season well with salt and pepper.

Pour the mixture into the greased brownie tin and smooth it out so it is the same thickness throughout. Push a large sheet of cling film onto the surface of the mixture, smoothing it out so that no air is trapped. Chill in the fridge for 2 hours, or until set and firm to the touch.

Set a large saucepan of salted water over a medium heat and bring to a boil. Add the broad beans for 1 minute. Drain and refresh under cold water. Use your nails to help pierce through the thick grey skins and pop out the green beans from within – it's so much nicer to eat broad beans like this and it's worth the effort, we promise. Set aside.

TIME: 30 MINUTES + CHILLING **SERVES: 4** **GLUTEN-FREE**

METHOD CONTINUED

When the chickpea gnocchi mixture is set, remove it from the fridge and tip it out onto a chopping board. Cut into small thumb-sized pieces.

Set a large frying pan over a medium heat, add the oil and fry the gnocchi for 3–4 minutes until golden on all sides – the pieces can be delicate until they develop a crust, so allow them to fry without stirring too often. Depending on the size of your pan, you may need to fry the gnocchi in batches.

Once golden, throw in the broad beans and remaining butter and toss well to coat. Add the lemon zest and juice and swill the pan around to emulsify the buttery lemon sauce – you may need an extra splash of water here.

Serve with a generous handful of Parmesan, a grind of black pepper and basil leaves to garnish.

TIP

You can make the panisse up to 4 days in advance before frying, so it's a great make-ahead dinner party number, and it also makes great chips if you have any leftovers.

Pork Chops with Peaches + Padron

METHOD

Preheat the oven to 200°C fan.

Set a large ovenproof frying pan or casserole dish over a medium-high heat. Season the pork chops generously with flaky salt. When the pan is hot, cook the chops fat-side down to start rendering out all of the delicious porky flavour. You can prop them up together against the side of the pan where they can render away happily for 5–6 minutes.

When plenty of pork fat has rendered out of the chops, place the peaches cut-side down in the pan to caramelise with the pork for 2–3 minutes. Once they're nicely coloured, remove them and transfer to a plate.

Once the pork chops have a caramelised fat cap, crank up the heat and sear them on each side for 4–5 minutes. The heat should be really high at this stage; embrace the hissing and crackling, it's flavour!

Remove the pork chops from the pan, leaving behind the residual pork fat.

Take the hot pan off the heat and chuck in the peppers. Roll them around in the fat. They should hiss and crackle and start to blister – hit them with a big pinch of salt. Once blistered, remove from the pan.

Set the pan back over a medium-low heat and add the garlic, cook until fragrant, then add the whole jar of beans (including the liquid) and half of the sherry vinegar to the pan. Bring to a gentle simmer.

THE DISH

A marriage of flavour that works every single time. You could swap the peaches for plums or nectarines if they're more your style – any stone fruit will work beautifully. The sweet and sour notes from the fruit and the sharp vinegar come into their own when paired with a rich, fatty pork chop.

INGREDIENTS

2 large thick-cut, bone-in **pork chops**
2 large ripe **peaches**, de-stoned and halved
250g **padron peppers**
6 **garlic cloves**, finely sliced
1 x 600g jar of **white beans**
4–5 tbsp **sherry vinegar**
salt and **black pepper**

TIME: 45 MINUTES   SERVES: 4   GLUTEN-FREE

Nestle the peaches, cut-side up, in the pan and pop the pork chops and padron peppers on top. Drizzle with the remaining vinegar and bang the whole lot into the oven for 8–10 minutes.

The pork chops are cooked when they are relatively firm with a subtle bounce. If you have a meat thermometer, it should read around 52°C. Pull the pork chops out and leave to rest for 4–5 minutes.

Carve the chops off the bone and cut the pork into thick slices. Arrange over the pan or on a platter, finish with a grind of black pepper and serve the whole dish family-style.

The cooking times here are for really fat pork chops – if yours are thinner, you may only need to cook them for 1–2 minutes on each side in the pan.

Vinegar Chicken + Chips

THE DISH

Malt vinegar doesn't get enough airtime. We've all got it lying around in our cupboards, and it makes the chicken in this dish insanely tender. Throw in some sweet red onions and you've got a killer sweet and sour chicken gravy to accompany an absolute classic. This is chicken and chips done right.

INGREDIENTS

4 skin-on **chicken thigh and leg portions**
200ml **malt vinegar**
3 tbsp **dark brown sugar**
6 **thyme sprigs**
1kg **floury potatoes**, such as Maris Piper
3 small **red onions**, sliced into wedges
4 tbsp **olive oil**
salt

METHOD

Add the chicken, vinegar, sugar, leaves from 4 thyme sprigs and a big pinch of salt into a freezer bag, shake to combine and leave to marinate for an hour (outside of the fridge).

Meanwhile, bring a large saucepan of water to a boil over a medium-high heat. Cook the potatoes for 10–12 minutes, or until just tender. You can also do this in the microwave by piercing the potatoes all over and cooking on high for 10 minutes until soft-ish when you squeeze them. Set aside to cool.

Preheat the oven to 180°C fan. Add the onion wedges to a deep baking tray and nestle the marinated chicken legs on top – make sure you pour over all the marinade, too. Slice the par-cooked potatoes into chips/wedges (how many you get from each potato will depend on the size of your potato) and carefully lay on a baking tray. Drizzle over the olive oil and gently turn them to coat evenly.

Add both trays to the oven, with the chicken on the bottom shelf. After 30 minutes, baste the chicken, then return to the oven on the top shelf for 10–15 minutes more until the skin is golden and burnished and the chicken is cooked through.

Remove the chicken from the oven, giving the chips a further 10 minutes on the top shelf until golden and crisp while the chicken rests.

Remove the chicken and onions from the baking tray – you should be left with quite a lot of thin liquid. To make this into a thicker gravy, whisk it vigorously until it emulsifies.

Serve the chicken and chips with the gravy and an extra sprinkling of thyme leaves.

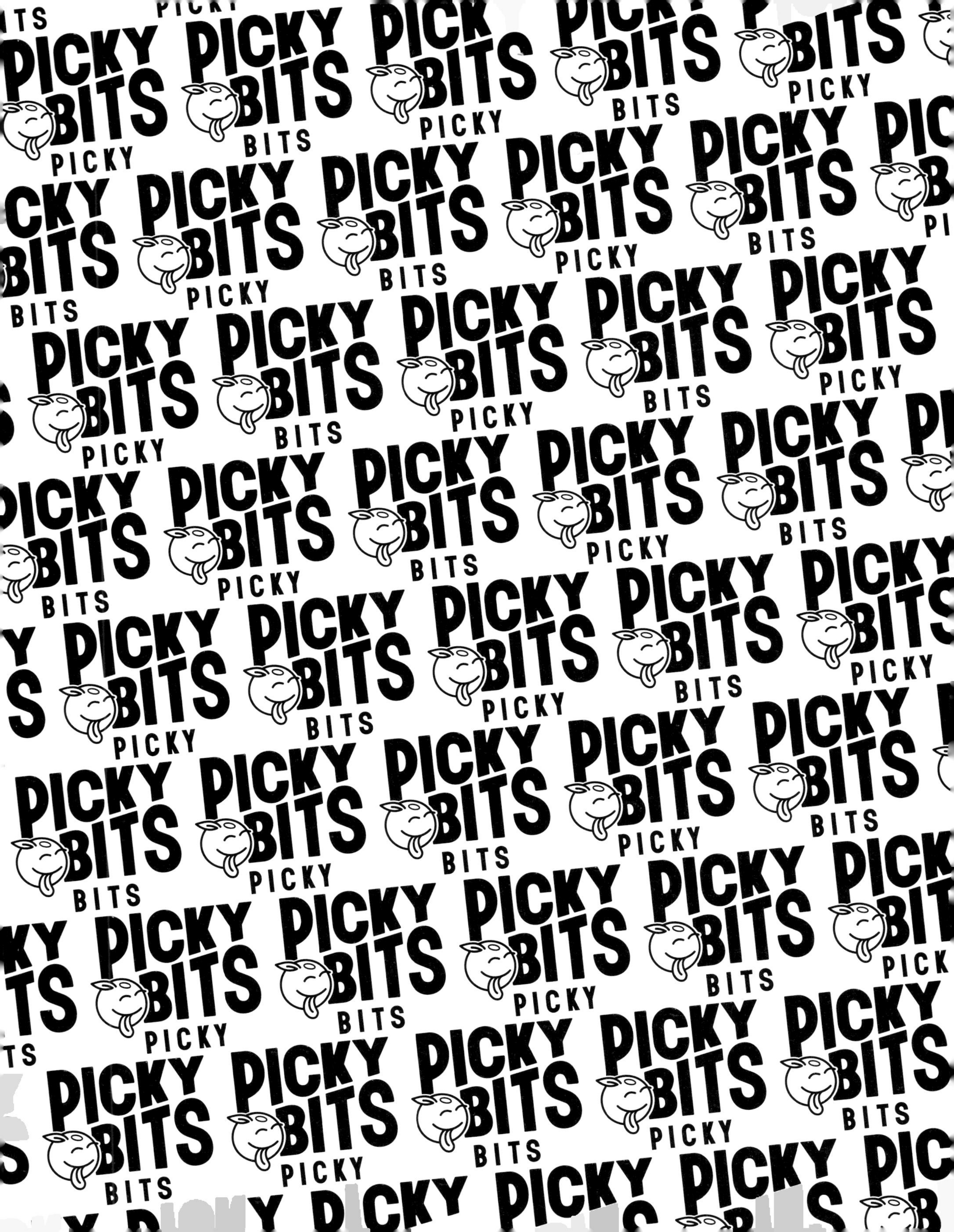
PICKY
BITS

Hummus with Zingy Courgettes

THE DISH

We think this tastes ten times better with super creamy shop-bought hummus, but feel free to experiment with flavoured hummus, too – there are some excellent smoked versions on the market that would work just as well.

INGREDIENTS

2 **pitta breads**
4 tbsp **extra virgin olive oil**
3 **courgettes**, sliced thinly into rounds
1 tbsp **sumac**, plus extra to sprinkle
200g **hummus**
125g **pitted queen olives**, roughly chopped
50g **pomegranate seeds**
salt and **black pepper**

METHOD

Toast the pitta breads until crisp, about 2 minutes. Cut them into tortilla-crisp-sized triangles, toss with 1 tablespoon of olive oil and season to taste.

Meanwhile, set a large frying pan over a medium heat, add the remaining olive oil and the courgettes and fry for 6–7 minutes until some pieces are golden and crisp, and they are all tender. Sprinkle over the sumac and season generously. Turn the heat off.

Add the hummus to a large shallow bowl and spread it around up to the edges. Top with the courgettes, olives and pomegranate seeds. Sprinkle with a little extra sumac and serve with the pitta chips.

TIME: 20 MINUTES   **SERVES: 4**   **VEGAN**

Hispi Pakoras with Mango Chutney

THE DISH

You can use all sorts of vegetables for a pakora – this batter can be used to coat onions, fish, sweetcorn, salad leaves – you name it, you can fry it. Here, we've used finely shredded hispi cabbage to create a snackable plate of craggy fritters.

INGREDIENTS

150g **hispi cabbage** (also known as sweetheart or pointed cabbage in the supermarket), very finely shredded
3 **spring onions**, finely sliced
a small handful of **coriander**, stalks and leaves finely chopped, a few sprigs saved for garnish
150g **chickpea (gram) flour**, plus 3 tbsp
1 tbsp **garam masala**
vegetable oil, to fry
mango chutney, to serve
salt

METHOD

Add the cabbage, spring onions and the chopped coriander to a large bowl. Add the chickpea flour and the garam masala with a big pinch of salt. Mix well to combine.

Add 6 tablespoons of water, stir and you should be left with a dry-ish mixture (not a batter) that clings on to the cabbage, resembling damp crumbs. When you squeeze a handful together, it should stick.

At this point, add the 3 extra tablespoons of chickpea flour – this helps the pakoras get really crispy.

Add the oil to a deep saucepan so that it comes no more than halfway up the sides and set over a high heat. When the oil shimmers, you're ready to fry.

Grab small, golf-ball-sized handfuls of the mixture, gently squeeze together, then drop straight into the oil – wispy bits will fling off the sides, and that's fine!

Fry for 2–3 minutes until golden and crisp. Remove with a slotted spoon, drain on kitchen paper and season again with salt. Repeat with all the remaining mixture.

Serve with the coriander sprigs and mango chutney for dipping.

Jalapeño Bottle Caps

THE DISH

Deep-fried pickled jalapeños. You can't get better than a fistful of these with an ice-cold beer. Crispy, spicy and completely moreish. The ultimate bar snack.

INGREDIENTS

1 x 200g jar of **pickled jalapeños**, plus 100ml pickling liquid
60g **plain flour**, plus 4 tbsp
vegetable oil, to fry
2 tsp **fajita seasoning**
a small handful of **coriander** leaves, finely chopped
150g **soured cream**
1 **lime**, zested
salt and **black pepper**

METHOD

Drain the jalapeños, reserving 100ml of the pickling liquid they came in. Blot them well with kitchen paper to dry and toss them with the 4 tablespoons of flour until coated.

Add the oil to a medium-sized deep saucepan so that it comes no more than halfway up the sides and set over a high heat until the temperature reaches 180°C (use a cooking thermometer).

Pour the reserved pickling liquid into a large bowl with 60g plain flour and the fajita seasoning. Dip the jalapeños in the batter, then scoop them out using a fork and transfer straight to the hot oil.

Working in batches, fry for 2 minutes until golden and crisp, then remove and drain on kitchen paper to soak up any excess oil.

In a small bowl, mix most of the coriander (saving some for garnish), soured cream and lime zest. Cut the zested lime into wedges.

Serve the jalapeños with a sprinkle of salt, pepper and the remaining coriander, with the dipping sauce and lime wedges alongside.

TIME: 20 MINUTES   **SERVES: 6**   **VEGGIE**

Sesame
Beef Toast

THE DISH

This is our meaty take on prawn toast. It sounds like a lot, and it is. But it's also crispy, addictive and totally delicious. Skip the takeaway and have a go at making these at home.

INGREDIENTS

3 **spring onions**, finely chopped
500g **beef mince** (20% fat)
1 **egg**
3 tbsp **soy sauce**, plus extra to serve
vegetable oil, to fry, plus 1 tbsp if needed
100g **sesame seeds**
6 slices of thick, soft **white bread**,
    quartered diagonally
salt and **black pepper**

METHOD

Add most of the spring onions (reserving some for garnish) to a food processor with the beef mince, egg and soy sauce. Season with salt and pepper and pulse until you have a smooth paste. If it seems dry, you may need to add a tablespoon of oil.

Pour your sesame seeds onto a shallow plate and set aside.

Spread a few tablespoons of your paste onto each slice of bread, going right up to the edges, then dip the paste side of each slice into the sesame seeds to completely cover the beef mixture.

Pour oil into a large saucepan or wok to come halfway up the sides and set over a high heat until the temperature reaches 180°C (use a cooking thermometer, or you can test with a wooden chopstick by dipping it in the oil; if you see steady bubbles around the stick, the oil is hot enough).

Fry the bread slices for 2–3 minutes until golden brown – flipping if you can (although sometimes they will flip themselves back over!). Work in batches so you don't overcrowd the oil.

Remove the beef toast with a slotted spoon and drain any excess oil on kitchen paper.

Garnish with the reserved spring onions and serve the toasts with extra soy sauce for dunking.

TIME: 45 MINUTES

SERVES: 6

Prawn Rice Paper Dumplings

THE DISH

Great things come in small packages and these dumplings pack an unbelievable amount of flavour. Plus, they're deceptively easy to cook. Frying your dumps until they're golden gives you that coveted crisp-yet-chewy texture that you'll be thinking about well after they've been polished off.

INGREDIENTS

150g **carrots**, cut into matchsticks
3 **spring onions**, thinly sliced
a small handful of **coriander**, stalks and leaves kept separate
12 **rice paper wrappers**
200g **cooked king prawns**
4 tbsp **vegetable oil**
4 tbsp **sweet chilli sauce**

METHOD

In a large bowl, mix together the carrots, spring onions and coriander stalks.

Clear your work surface and get a large shallow bowl of water.

Briefly dunk a rice paper wrapper in the water, then transfer to a clean chopping board – don't worry if it is not fully bendy yet, it will be malleable by the time you roll it!

Place 3–4 prawns in a row along the centre of the wrapper, then pile a small handful of the carrot filling on top. Fold in the opposite sides of the circle, tuck the bottom side up and over, then roll to create a tight log parcel. Repeat for each dumpling. Transfer to a baking paper-lined baking tray – don't let them touch as they can be quite sticky at this stage.

Heat the vegetable oil in a frying pan set over a medium heat and, working in batches, fry the dumplings for 2 minutes on each side until golden and crisp.

Meanwhile, mix half of the chopped coriander leaves with the sweet chilli sauce in a small dipping bowl.

Add the fried dumplings to a serving plate, scatter with the remaining coriander and dunk in the sweet chilli sauce.

Smashed Plantain + Scotch Bonnet Jam

THE DISH

This spicy number is perfect if you're in the market for a delicious and impressive snack. We've gone with ripe, sweet plantains here but you can use green, unripe plantains for an even crispier result. Highly eatable.

INGREDIENTS

1 **scotch bonnet chilli**
1 x 465g jar of **roasted red peppers**
4 tbsp **ginger garlic paste**
65g **caster sugar**
vegetable oil, to fry
4 ripe **plantains**, chopped into 3cm chunks
2 **limes**, cut into wedges
salt and **black pepper**

METHOD

Remove the stem from the scotch bonnet. Place in a food processor with the red peppers (brine included), ginger garlic paste and sugar. Blitz until finely chopped.

Transfer to a saucepan set over a medium heat. Cook until thickened and jammy, 5–10 minutes, then season with salt and pepper and leave to cool.

Meanwhile, fill a wide, deep saucepan halfway with the vegetable oil and set over a high heat until the temperature reaches 160°C (use a cooking thermometer to check). Work in batches, frying the plantain until golden, about 3–5 minutes.

Remove the plantain chunks with a slotted spoon and transfer to a chopping board to cool slightly, then gently flatten each piece with a ramekin until wide and thin.

Working in batches, fry the plantain pieces again until deeply golden brown all over, then drain on kitchen paper and season with salt. They will crisp up as they drain.

To serve, spread lots of the jam on the base of a plate. Top with the crispy smashed plantain and finish with a sprinkling of salt and the lime wedges to squeeze.

TIP

If using unripe plantain, you may need to heat the oil to 180°C.

Zingy Chilli Meatballs

METHOD

To make the meatballs, mix the ginger garlic paste with the pork mince and coriander stalks in a bowl. Season with salt and pepper and mix to combine.

Form the mixture into golf ball-sized meatballs, then chill in the fridge for 15 minutes.

Meanwhile, make the sauce. Place the sweet chilli sauce in a bowl. Add the ginger garlic paste, lime zest and juice and mix to combine. Set aside for later.

Add the vegetable oil to a large frying pan set over a high heat. Cook the meatballs until browned and cooked through, around 3 minutes per side, then remove from the pan. You may need to fry the meatballs in 2 batches if your frying pan isn't big enough so that the pan doesn't become overcrowded.

Add the sweet chilli mix sauce and cook for 2–3 minutes until bubbly and sticky, then return the meatballs to the pan and toss well to coat.

Plate up with extra lime wedges and garnish with the coriander sprigs to serve.

THE DISH

Want the ultimate dinner party snack? We've got you. These quick and easy marinated pork meatballs, which we've tossed in a sticky sweet chilli glaze, are the perfect nibble to serve up to your guests.

INGREDIENTS

FOR THE MEATBALLS
2 tbsp **ginger garlic paste**
800g **pork mince** (10% fat or more preferable)
a small handful of **coriander**, stalks finely chopped, leaves picked in small sprigs
1 tbsp **vegetable oil**
salt and **black pepper**

FOR THE SAUCE
250g **sweet chilli sauce**
3 tbsp **ginger garlic paste**
2 **limes**, zested and juiced, plus extra wedges to serve

TIME: 30 MINUTES + CHILLING   **SERVES: 4**   **GLUTEN-FREE**   235

Courgette + Halloumi Fritters

THE DISH

Everyone loves a tasty little fritter. These golden nugs manage to stay incredibly crispy thanks to a combo of grated halloumi and gram flour – a beautifully nutty, and surprisingly gluten-free, flour made from chickpeas. Swap out the parsley for coriander or dill, if you prefer.

INGREDIENTS

3 **courgettes**, coarsely grated
150g **halloumi**, coarsely grated
100g **chickpea (gram) flour**
1 tbsp **Aleppo pepper** or **chilli flakes**,
  plus extra to serve
a bunch of **flat leaf parsley** leaves, finely
  chopped and a few sprigs reserved
vegetable oil, to fry
150g **tzatziki**
salt

METHOD

Put the grated courgettes in a sieve set over a bowl and season with a pinch of salt. Give it all a toss, then leave to sit for 20 minutes.

Squeeze all the excess liquid out of your courgettes – use a clean tea towel, pile the courgette into the centre and gather up the corners, then wring out the moisture. Place the dried courgette in a bowl with the halloumi, chickpea flour, Aleppo pepper and the chopped parsley. Give it a really good mix. Form your mixture into 12 evenly-sized patties.

Set a frying pan over a high heat and pour in a generous glug of vegetable oil. Carefully fry the fritters in batches, for about 3 minutes on each side. They should be dark golden and crisp on the outside, tender on the inside. Lift out of the pan and drain on a plate lined with kitchen paper while you fry the rest.

Serve with tzatziki sprinkled with extra Aleppo pepper and the parsley sprigs scattered over.

Chipotle Polenta Fries

THE DISH

If you aren't yet a polenta convert, these fries might just give you the push you need. We've switched up the classic Italian flavours by adding in a dollop of chipotle paste. Crispy exterior. Molten, spicy middles. Dunked in chipotle mayo. It doesn't get better than that.

INGREDIENTS

375g **quick-cook polenta**
60g **Parmesan**, grated
50g **salted butter**
3 tbsp **chipotle paste**
150g **mayonnaise**
vegetable oil, to fry
a handful of **coriander**, leaves finely chopped
salt and **black pepper**

You will need a 20x20cm baking dish.

METHOD

Line a square baking dish, around 20x20cm, with cling film.

Pour 1 litre of water into a large saucepan. Bring to a boil over a medium-high heat, then add 300g of the polenta, whisking vigorously as you pour to ensure that it doesn't clump. Keep whisking while it simmers.

After a couple of minutes, when the mixture has thickened, add 50g of Parmesan. Add the butter and 2 tablespoons of chipotle paste, then generously season with salt and pepper. Whisk until combined.

Pour the mixture into the lined baking dish, then leave to chill in the fridge for an hour until firm to the touch.

Meanwhile, put the mayonnaise with the remaining chipotle paste in a bowl and mix to make the dipping sauce. Set aside.

Turn the chilled polenta out onto a chopping board and cut into 2.5cm-thick chips. Dip each one in the remaining polenta to coat.

Set a frying pan over a high heat and add a generous glug of oil. Add the polenta fries one by one and fry for 3–4 minutes on each side until they are golden and crispy.

Arrange on a serving plate and sprinkle with a little more Parmesan and coriander leaves to garnish. Serve up while still hot alongside the chipotle mayo for dipping.

TIME: 45 MINUTES + CHILLING   **MAKES: 25**   **GLUTEN-FREE**

Burnt Chilli, Tomato + Ricotta Dip

METHOD

Set a frying pan or griddle pan over a high heat. Add the chillies and cook for 7 minutes until the skins are black and charred, turning every so often. Alternatively, char them directly over the flame of a gas hob.

Allow the chillies to cool slightly, then cut a few slices from one chilli and reserve for garnish. Remove the skins from the chillies. Scrape out the seeds, then roughly chop the flesh.

Put the chopped chillies into a small food processor and add the sun-dried tomatoes, paprika and 4 tablespoons of olive oil. Blitz to a thick, smooth sauce, then season to taste with salt.

Add the ricotta to a big bowl along with the lemon juice, 2 tablespoons olive oil and a pinch of salt. Whisk until you have a smooth, creamy sauce.

Spoon the ricotta sauce into a serving bowl, then swoosh a spoon around the top to create a bit of a well. Top with a big dollop of burnt red chilli sauce and scatter with the chilli slices. Finish with black pepper and serve with crisps.

THE DISH

Your new favourite dip. Spicy, smoky chilli swirled through whipped ricotta is a real crowd-pleaser. We like dipping crisps into this bad boy, but you can dunk whatever you like. You'll get an extra bit of burnt chilli salsa from this, which can be stored in the fridge for a couple of days.

INGREDIENTS

3 **red chillies**
125g **sun-dried tomatoes**
½ tsp **sweet smoked paprika**
6 tbsp **olive oil**
250g **ricotta**
½ **lemon**, juiced
a bag of **salty crisps**, to serve
salt and **black pepper**

TIME: 20 MINUTES   SERVES: 4   VEGGIE, GLUTEN-FREE

6 Thrown-Together Bites

There are myriad ingredients we keep in our kitchen to make sure we've always got easy access to delicious quick nibbles. A lot of ingredients hardly need any sprucing up to be incredibly satisfying and, dare we say it, impressive. Here are a few stellar combos to try out as canapés when you have your mates over.

1. FISHY FORMULAS

Tinned and long-life fish are infinitely customisable and good for you, too.
- Skewer anchovies, olives and guindilla chilli peppers onto a cocktail stick for a classic Spanish Gilda.
- Lay a couple of sardines to rest on a slice of sourdough with thinly sliced red onion, dill and lots of lemon juice and zest.
- Slice a cucumber and load up each round with a medley of mackerel pâté, chopped cornichons, sliced radishes and finely chopped parsley.
- Roast some new potatoes before splitting them open and dolloping over soured cream. Top with smoked salmon, capers and crispy onions.

2. CHEESE + FRUIT

It's an almighty combo. If you don't know, now you know.
- Split open a handful of fat dates and stuff them with goat's cheese and halved walnuts. Bake your stuffed dates for 10 minutes at 180°C fan, then sprinkle with tarragon.
- Score figs and stuff to the brim with Gorgonzola. Scatter over some hazelnuts and bake for 8 minutes at 180°C fan, until the cheese has melted. Drizzle with balsamic vinegar or truffle oil.
- Load up crostini with creamy Taleggio, gossamer-thin slices of pear, thyme leaves and a drizzle of hot honey.
- Crumble some feta into thick Greek yoghurt and get ready to spread that dairy dream team on toast. Top with chopped dried apricots, a drizzle of honey and lots of cracked black pepper.

3. QUICK DIPS

When in doubt, get the crisps out.
- Make a quick and spicy tzatziki by grating half a cucumber into some yoghurt and stirring in a crushed garlic clove, chopped dill, lemon juice and plenty of Tabasco.
- Finely chop some mango, red onion, coriander and red chilli. Add the juice of 2–3 limes, and you've got a sweet and zesty salsa on your hands.
- Blitz the flesh of an avocado with soured cream, pickled jalapeños, chives and lime juice for an instant crema.
- Blend pre-cooked beetroots with hummus and drizzle over crispy chilli oil and a sprinkle of coriander.

4. OLIVES

We firmly believe that there is no one in the world who *actually* hates olives. Just people who haven't grown up yet.

- Peel and roughly chop some oranges, stuff them inside of plump green olives and sprinkle over dried oregano and lots of extra virgin olive oil.
- Finely chop pickled jalapeños and combine with cream cheese. Stuff your spicy cream cheese inside some olives, roll them in breadcrumbs and deep fry.
- Spread black olive tapenade on crostini and top with sliced jarred roasted red peppers and Manchego.
- Chop up some olives, preserved lemons and fresh oregano. Spoon over a torn burrata ball for a guaranteed good time.

5. PICKLES

We're not picky about our pickles – anything remotely vinegary and we're in.

- Wrap prosciutto around a blob of cream cheese with a few cornichons. Bonus points if you use those little pickled onions in the jar, too.
- Pop a few slices of avocado on a prawn cracker or sesame cracker and load it up with kimchi. Sprinkle with sesame seeds and a squeeze of lime. Sorted.
- Paw a good amount of sauerkraut onto crostini and top with chorizo slices, a dollop of crème fraîche and parsley.
- Toss sushi ginger with edamame, mango and chopped cucumber. Dress with soy sauce and sesame oil for a quick poke-style salsa.

6. PUFF PASTRY

Honestly, you wouldn't believe the things you can do with a roll of puff pastry. The list is endless.

- Spread tikka paste onto a few squares of puff pastry and layer up with sliced coins of courgette before showering with nigella seeds and chopped fresh coriander. Fold the edges over and bake at 180°C fan. until golden.
- Cut puff pastry into squares and mix in a bowl with grated halloumi, tomatoes, chopped fresh parsley and dried oregano. Stuff the mixture into a 12-hole muffin tin and bake at 180°C fan until you have golden pull-apart muffins.
- Lob some gochujang onto a sheet of puff pastry and spread it out roughly, cut it into strips and twirl it into twists. Finish with sesame seeds and bake at 180°C fan until golden.
- Cut puff pastry into rectangles, spread with passata and crumble over 'nduja and feta. Bake at 180°C fan until golden.

Curried Coronation Chickpea Dip

THE DISH

Whether you're treating it as a creamy dip or as an epic sandwich filling, this delivers British nostalgia by the bucketload. Try scooping it up with poppadoms or veggie crudités. You won't regret it.

INGREDIENTS

2 x 400g tins of **chickpeas**, drained and rinsed
5 tbsp **vegan mayonnaise**
2 tsp **curry powder**
3 tbsp **mango chutney**
a handful of **crispy onions**
a handful of **coriander** leaves
salt and **black pepper**

METHOD

In a bowl, combine the chickpeas with the mayonnaise, curry powder and 2 tablespoons of mango chutney.

Use the back of the spoon to slightly crush roughly half of the chickpeas against the side of the bowl as you give it a good mix. Season to taste.

Plate up with an extra dollop of mango chutney and top with the crispy onions and coriander leaves.

TIME: 5 MINUTES   SERVES: 4   VEGAN   245

Crisp-y
Fish Nuggets

THE DISH

Coating fish pieces in your favourite packet of crisps is a game-changer that'll give you so much salty, crunchy goodness. Try out different types of crisps to switch things up. We like pickled onion Monster Munch and Frazzles. But you do you.

INGREDIENTS

2 x 25g packets of **salt and vinegar crisps**
6 tbsp **mayonnaise**
250g skinless and boneless **cod fillets**,
    cut into 3cm chunks
vegetable oil, to fry
1 tbsp **capers**, finely chopped
a small bunch of **chives**, finely chopped
1 **lemon**
salt and **black pepper**

METHOD

Pour the crisps into a sandwich bag and smash with a rolling pin until they are crumbs.

Add 3 tablespoons of mayonnaise to a small bowl, coat the cod chunks in the mayonnaise, using a spoon to get rid of any excess (you only want a thin film), then add the fish to the sandwich bag in batches. Pinch closed at the top and shake well to coat in the crumbs.

Set the coated chunks of fish aside on a baking tray as you work, until all the fish has a crumb coating.

Set a saucepan over a medium heat and pour in 3cm of vegetable oil. Heat the oil to 170°C (use a cooking thermometer to check).

Meanwhile, in a small bowl add the remaining mayonnaise, the capers, most of the chives (reserving some to garnish) and the juice of ½ a lemon. Season to taste.

Deep fry the fish chunks for 2 minutes in the hot oil until golden and cooked through – be gentle with them as they fry, you don't want to nudge off the coating. Drain on a plate lined with kitchen paper and season with salt.

Serve the nuggets with the lemon caper mayo, any remaining chives scattered over and the other half of the lemon for an extra zingy squeeze. Finish with a sprinkling of salt.

Fish Sauce Wings

THE DISH

These sticky, savoury wings pack a powerful umami punch. We promise, you won't be able to stop at just one. Or two. Or three.

INGREDIENTS

FOR THE WINGS
4 **garlic cloves**, crushed
150ml **fish sauce** (check the label if making gluten-free)
200g **light brown sugar**
1kg **whole chicken wings**
150g **cornflour**, plus 2 tsp for the marinade
vegetable oil, to fry

FOR THE TOPPING
vegetable oil, to fry
100g **raw peanuts**, finely chopped
2 **garlic cloves**, crushed
salt and **black pepper**

METHOD

In a large mixing bowl, place the garlic, fish sauce, sugar and 200ml of water. Whisk until the sugar is dissolved. This is the marinade.

Add the wings to the marinade and toss to coat. Leave to marinate in the fridge for at least 1 hour, or overnight if you have the time.

Meanwhile, for the topping, fill a small saucepan halfway with vegetable oil and set over a medium heat. Add the peanuts and cook for 5 minutes, or until golden – it can be quite bubbly in the pan, so give it a swirl around to get a good visual on it.

Add the garlic and cook for 1 minute, or until fragrant, then drain. Season with salt and pepper, toss to coat and leave to cool in a sieve.

For the chicken wings, put the 150g of cornflour in a deep roasting tin and coat each wing before setting aside.

Transfer the marinade to a small saucepan. Dissolve the remaining 2 teaspoons of cornflour in 1 tablespoon of water and add to the saucepan.

Bring to a boil over a medium heat, then reduce the heat to low and simmer for 5 minutes. Remove the saucepan from the heat.

Fill a large, wide pan halfway with vegetable oil and heat it to 170°C (use a cooking thermometer). Working in batches, fry the wings until golden, crisp and cooked through, about 10 minutes.

Toss the wings in the sauce, then plate up, topped with the garlicky peanuts.

Cherry + Tomato Bruschetta

THE DISH

Cherries and tomatoes are a surprisingly beautiful combination – especially in the height of summer when they're both bursting with natural sweetness. Use more of one when the other's out of season.

INGREDIENTS

2 **preserved lemons**
150g **cherry tomatoes**, halved or quartered
100g **cherries**, halved and pitted
100g **feta**
4 sprigs of **oregano**
4 tbsp **extra virgin olive oil**, plus extra
    to drizzle
2 slices of **sourdough**
salt and **black pepper**

METHOD

Halve the preserved lemons, scoop out the inner flesh and discard it. Finely chop the rinds and add to a bowl.

Add the cherry tomatoes and cherries to the bowl.

Crumble in the feta and pick the leaves from 3 of the sprigs of oregano and add to the bowl. Season well with salt and pepper and pour in the olive oil. Mix well to combine and set aside to marinate while you make the toast (you could leave it in the fridge overnight if prepping ahead of time).

Toast the sourdough, then top with the cherry and tomato mixture. Garnish with the remaining oregano leaves and an extra drizzle of olive oil. Finish with a grind of black pepper.

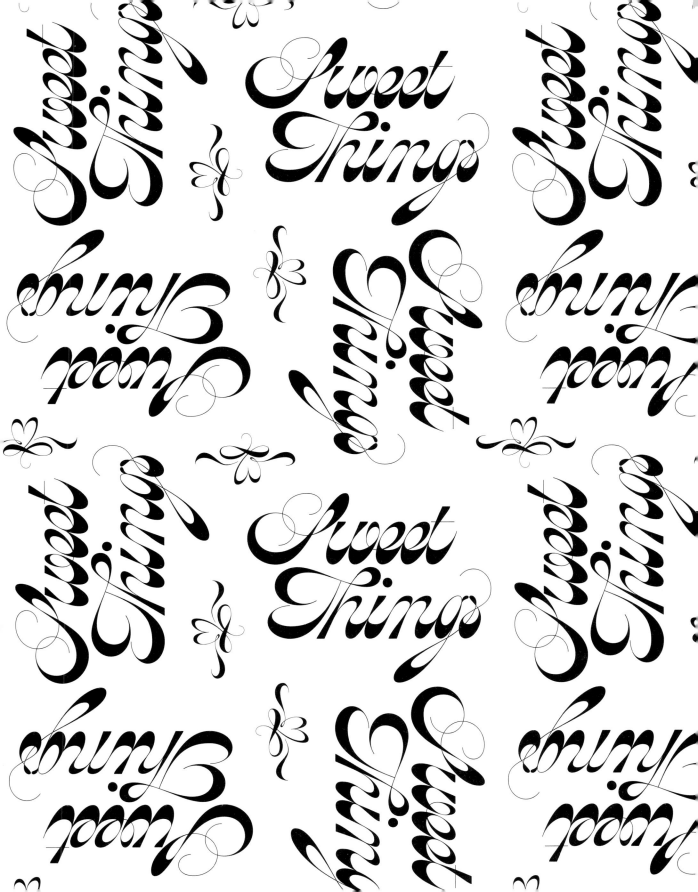

Cardamom + Apricot Tarts

THE DISH

Adding more egg to shop-bought custard means you can make pastéis-de-nata-style custard tarts with a handful of ingredients. We are obsessed with cardamom and it brings a deeply aromatic flavour to these cute little pastries.

INGREDIENTS

1 x 500g block of **shortcrust pastry**
5 **green cardamom pods**, pods split open,
  seeds separated
250g **shop-bought custard**
2 **egg yolks**
6 tsp **apricot jam**
10g **shelled pistachios**, finely chopped

You will need a 12-hole muffin tin.

TIP

You'll have some extra pastry and filling, which will keep in the fridge for 3–4 days.

METHOD

Preheat the oven to 180°C fan.

Roll out the pastry between 2 sheets of baking paper to roughly the thickness of a pound coin. Use a large glass (like a pint glass), around 8–9cm in diameter, and cut around with a sharp knife to make 12 pastry discs. You may need to re-roll the pastry after the first batch to make enough. Push the pastry discs into a 12-hole muffin tin and press up against the sides, leaving a 1cm rim at the top.

Cut 12 large squares from the baking paper you used before and scrunch each one up into a paper ball. Smooth out the balls and place 1 baking paper square in each hole. Tip in enough baking beans to weigh down the paper in each hole and put into the oven for 10 minutes.

Meanwhile, put the cardamom seeds in a pestle and mortar and bash until ground, or use a sharp knife to finely chop them. Add to a medium-sized mixing jug with the custard and egg yolks. Whisk well to combine.

After the pastry has been in the oven for 10 minutes, carefully remove the baking paper and baking beans. Reduce the oven temperature to 150°C fan.

Add half a teaspoon of apricot jam to the base of each pastry case. Pour the custard into each tart to fill. Return to the oven to bake for 15 minutes until the custard has set – if you wiggle the tin, the filling should have a slight quiver, but not a violent jiggle.

Allow to cool in the tin for 10 minutes before transferring to a wire rack to cool completely. Sprinkle with chopped pistachios and serve.

'Negroni' Jelly + Ice Cream

THE DISH

Jelly and ice cream for grown-ups. Olive oil might seem like an odd ingredient; however, not only does it look gorgeous but it also adds an interesting grassy note to the recipe that offsets the sweetness like a dream. Think of it like adding a pinch of salt to a cake or brownie mix.

INGREDIENTS

6–7 **blood oranges**
3 **gelatine leaves**
35g **caster sugar**
25ml **Campari**
ice cream, to serve
a handful of **salted roasted shelled pistachios**, roughly chopped
extra virgin olive oil, for drizzling

You will need 2 small jelly moulds or other suitable containers (approx. 200ml).

METHOD

Halve and juice 5 of the blood oranges to get roughly 400ml of juice. Segment the remaining oranges, squeezing any extra juice from the cores over the segments to keep them juicy.

Submerge the gelatine leaves in icy cold water for 5 minutes, until soft.

Meanwhile, set a saucepan over a low heat, add the sugar and 100ml of the fresh blood orange juice and bring to a low simmer.

Squeeze the excess water out of the gelatine and add to the hot juice and sugar, whisking until the gelatine is completely dissolved. Add the remaining blood orange juice and the Campari.

Pour the mixture into the 2 jelly moulds, or another suitable container, and chill in the fridge for 3–4 hours until set.

Serve the jelly in cold bowls with the fresh blood orange segments, a heaping scoop of ice cream, a handful of pistachios and a drizzle of extra virgin olive oil.

SWAP

Make this all year round with regular oranges, of course!

TIME: 25 MINUTES + SETTING   SERVES: 2   GLUTEN-FREE

Chilli Chocolate Mousse

THE DISH

This rich, velvety mousse has become the stuff of legend at Mob HQ. Chilli might seem a rogue addition, but we promise it works. That said, the star of the show might just be the spicy candied pecans.

INGREDIENTS

FOR THE MOUSSE
100g **dark chocolate**, roughly chopped
1 tbsp **coconut oil**
250g **silken tofu**, drained
1 **red chilli**, deseeded if you prefer less heat, roughly chopped
80ml **maple syrup**
salt

FOR THE CHILLI CANDIED PECANS
1 tsp **coconut oil**
1 **red chilli**, deseeded if you prefer less heat, thinly sliced
75g **pecans**
4 tbsp **maple syrup**

You will need 6 ramekins or small glasses.

METHOD

Set a heatproof bowl over a saucepan of barely simmering water and keep at a low heat, making sure the water is not touching the base of the bowl. Add the chocolate and coconut oil, stirring constantly so it doesn't burn, until melted. Leave to cool slightly.

Add the tofu to a blender and blitz until fully liquidised, then add the melted chocolate mixture, red chilli, maple syrup and a pinch of salt. Taste for sweetness and add more maple syrup if you like.

Pour the mixture evenly into 6 ramekins or small glasses and chill for at least 45 minutes in the fridge.

Meanwhile, for the pecans, set a frying pan over a medium heat and add the coconut oil. Add the chilli and cook for 1 minute, then add the pecans and toast for another minute.

Add the maple syrup and cook until reduced and sticky, around 5 minutes.

Line a baking tray with baking paper and pour in the mixture. Leave to cool.

To serve, top the mousses with the spicy candied pecans and a final sprinkling of salt.

TIME: 20 MINUTES + CHILLING   SERVES: 6   VEGGIE, GLUTEN-FREE   259

White Chocolate + Tahini Cheesecake

THE DISH

This cheesecake has the perfect balance of sweet and salty. A creamy no-bake dessert that's easy to whip up in a flash, this is destined to become your go-to pud when having friends over.

INGREDIENTS

FOR THE BISCUIT BASE
130g **salted butter**, melted, plus extra for greasing
1 packet of **dark chocolate biscuits** (approx. 300g)

FOR THE CHEESECAKE
300g **white chocolate**, broken into pieces
120g **salted butter**
60g **tahini**
320g **cream cheese**
260g **double cream**

You will need a 20cm springform tin.

METHOD

Grease a 20cm springform tin and line with a circle of baking paper.

For the biscuit base, blitz the biscuits in a food processor, or add them to a sandwich bag and bash the living daylights out of them with a rolling pin to make fine crumbs.

Set 2–3 tablespoons of the biscuit crumbs to one side for later. Pour the rest into a bowl with the melted butter, mix together well, then tip into the prepared tin and press down with the back of a spoon to create the cheesecake base. Pop into the fridge to chill until set while you make the topping.

For the cheesecake, put the white chocolate and butter in a heatproof bowl and microwave in 30-second bursts, stirring after each interval, until totally melted together and smooth. Set aside to cool.

In a large bowl, use a hand whisk to mix together the tahini, cream cheese and double cream until soft peaks form.

Pour in the cooled melted white chocolate and butter mixture and whisk again to combine until soft peaks form.

Remove the tin from the fridge. Pour the mixture into the tin over the set biscuit base and sprinkle over the reserved biscuit crumbs. Return to the fridge for at least 3 hours to set, then serve in slices.

Grilled Peaches, Cream + Basil

METHOD

Set a griddle pan or frying pan over a medium-high heat and add a splash of vegetable oil.

Place the peaches cut-side down into the pan and cook for about 4 minutes, turning to get good colour all over. Remove from the heat and transfer to a small bowl.

In a large mixing bowl, add the double cream, vanilla bean paste and half of the honey. Whip until soft peaks form.

Chop or bash up the biscuits to the texture of large breadcrumbs. Add half to the cream and stir until just combined.

Separate the cream into 4 bowls or spoon onto a big serving platter and top with the peaches. Now sprinkle over the remaining biscuit crumbs, tear over the basil leaves and drizzle with the rest of the honey.

THE DISH

Grilling peaches is a great way to bring out their natural perfume and sweetness. We've layered them up with whipped cream, fragrant basil and honey for a simple summer-appropriate dessert.

INGREDIENTS

1 tbsp **vegetable oil**
4 **peaches**, de-stoned and quartered
500ml **double cream**
2 tsp **vanilla bean paste**
4 tbsp **honey**
10 **gingernut biscuits**
a handful of **basil** leaves

TIME: 15 MINUTES   **SERVES: 4**   **VEGGIE**

Tangerine
Tiramisu

THE DISH

This zesty twist on tiramisu is a great winter pud. It's alcohol-free, so everyone can enjoy it. Plus, there's no cooking involved. Just layer it up and pop it in the fridge. It literally couldn't be easier.

INGREDIENTS

4 **eggs**, whites and yolks separated
90g **caster sugar**
500g **mascarpone**
coffee grounds, to make 350ml strong coffee
200g **Savoiardi biscuits**
3 **tangerines**, zested and sliced into rounds

You will need an approx. 25x20cm dish.

METHOD

Put the egg whites into a mixing bowl or the bowl of a stand mixer. Add half of the sugar to the whites and whisk into soft peaks, then set aside.

Put the yolks into a small bowl and add the remaining half of the sugar, whisking until pale. Add the mascarpone and whisk again until smooth.

Carefully fold the egg whites into the mascarpone mixture a spoonful at a time, trying to knock out as little air as possible.

Brew 350ml of coffee, pour into a small dish and leave to cool slightly. Line a baking tray with kitchen paper.

Dip the Savoiardi biscuits into the coffee mix for about 3 seconds, then place on the tray with the kitchen paper.

Arrange the biscuits in a single layer across the base of an oven dish. Spread half of the mascarpone cream over the biscuits. Sprinkle half of the zest over the cream. Lay half of the tangerine slices over the cream layer.

Repeat, arranging the second layer of biscuits over the tangerines, spreading over the remaining mascarpone cream and then adding another layer of the tangerine slices. Sprinkle over the remaining zest.

Cover with cling film and chill in the fridge for at least 4 hours or overnight.

Cherry Cheesecake Cookies

METHOD

Add the cream cheese, butter, sugar and vanilla to a bowl and beat until light and fluffy using an electric whisk.

Add the flour and black pepper and stir by hand until just combined.

Cover with cling film and chill in the fridge for at least 3 hours or overnight until firm and set.

Preheat the oven to 180°C fan. Line a baking tray with baking paper.

Remove the mixture from the fridge and use a small ice cream scoop or 2 tablespoons to scoop out cookie dough balls the size of a walnut or ping pong ball. Space the balls out well on the baking tray (probably 8 cookies to 1 tray). Use your thumb or the back of a teaspoon to make a deep imprint in the centre of each cookie and fill each one with ½–1 teaspoon of cherry jam (depending on the size of your indent).

Bake for 10 minutes until golden at the edges, remove from the oven and leave on the tray for 5 minutes to firm up before transferring to a wire rack to cool fully. Repeat with the remaining batches of dough.

THE DISH

Black pepper lends these soft and delicate melt-in-your-mouth cookies a lovely tickle of spice – it goes so well with all sorts of jams, so play around with your favourite.

INGREDIENTS

120g **cream cheese**
120g **salted butter**, softened
150g **caster sugar**
½ tsp **vanilla extract**
150g **plain flour**
1 tsp freshly ground **black pepper**
7 tbsp **cherry jam**, to fill

TIME: 45 MINUTES + CHILLING   MAKES: 20   VEGGIE

Plum + Almond Cake

THE DISH

Think of this cake as a blank canvas that you can tweak and adapt with whatever fruit and toppings you like. Try apple slices with crumbled walnuts or pears with sprinkled demerara sugar. Go wild.

INGREDIENTS

5 tbsp **vegetable oil**, plus extra for greasing
220g **self-raising flour**
220g **caster sugar**
½ tsp **salt**
½ tbsp **white wine vinegar**
2 tsp **vanilla extract**
4 **plums**, de-stoned and thinly sliced into half moons
30g **flaked almonds**

You will need a 20x20cm brownie tin.

METHOD

Preheat the oven to 180°C fan. Grease a 20x20cm brownie tin. Cut 2 strips of baking paper and lay these over the base in a cross shape (this will make it easier to remove the cake later). Set aside.

In a large bowl, mix together the flour, sugar and salt. Add the oil, white wine vinegar and vanilla extract and mix to combine.

Add 220ml of water, whisking well to make a smooth batter until there are no more visible bits of dry flour.

Pour the batter into the prepared tin, then top with the fanned slices of plum. Sprinkle the surface with the flaked almonds.

Bake for 30–35 minutes, or until lightly golden on top, and when you prod a skewer or cocktail stick into the centre of the cake it comes out clean.

Allow to rest for 5 minutes to firm up a little before lifting the cake out of the tin using the baking paper. Allow to cool fully on a wire rack.

TIME: 45 MINUTES   SERVES: 9–12   VEGAN

6 Seasonal Fruit Stars

We're firm believers in trying to make the most of produce when it's in season – fruit and vegetables consumed at their peak are infinitely more delicious than their far-flung-farmed and imported counterparts. Not only that, but they're full of nutrients, too. It's a win-win, really. Here are some ideas about what to do with our favourite fruits from each season.

1. DECEMBER + JANUARY: CITRUS SEASON

Winter sees us come into full citrus swing. Clementines, mandarins, bergamot and grapefruits are all deliciously juicy and sweet around this time of the year. Try removing the peel and cutting your fruit into segments before coating them in a dark, dry caramel for an insanely quick dessert that tastes better the longer it sits. The combination of citrus with lovely shards of crunchy sugar is unreal.

2. FEBRUARY + MARCH: APPLES + PEARS

Think 'crumbles' and run with it. Fruits in this season are begging to be slowly stewed, coaxing out their natural sweetness. Apples and pears are dreamy when partnered with a few simple crunchy and creamy elements. Switch up your crumble topping by using granola or even crushing up cereal, like cornflakes, for some interesting crisp textures.

3. APRIL + MAY: RHUBARB + GOOSEBERRIES

Both of these fruits need a little bit of help to counteract their natural acidity. Try adding sugar and flavourings like hibiscus tea, vanilla or citrus, and cooking them down to make an array of compotes and jams. They'll keep for ages and you can taste their fleeting seasonal glory later in the year – it's like having a mini time machine in a jar.

4. JUNE + JULY:
ALL THE BERRIES

Berries in the summer are an absolute non-negotiable. When you taste them, you realise the berries you were eating year-round didn't even come close to their true taste. Most berries all work very harmoniously together – and summer is screaming out for a pavlova. Load up your pav with cream, cover it with cherries, strawberries and raspberries and then drizzle over a zigzag of passion fruit, tahini or date syrup.

5. AUGUST +
SEPTEMBER:
STONE FRUIT

Plums, peaches and nectarines are crying out for you to make a galette – and they taste even better when paired with cheese. We know it sounds odd but hear us out. Spread soft goat's cheese onto a base of puff pastry and layer on your in-season peaches, then scatter over some pecans. Fold the pastry at the edges, give it a lick of egg wash, sprinkle over demerara sugar and bake at 180°C fan until golden. Pair plums with a mild Gorgonzola and walnuts. Nectarines with crumbled feta and pine nuts. Heaven.

6. OCTOBER +
NOVEMBER:
QUINCE + CRANBERRIES

As soon as winter rolls around, we're going to lean hard into festive flavours. Poach quince in mixed spice, red wine and sugar. Serve it with heaps of vanilla ice cream and load on a bunch of pistachios. Eat it before the ice cream melts. Mix cranberries with candied citrus and dried fruit and bake them into crumble bars. A lot of people get scared by fruits they don't cook a lot, and we get it! Quince sounds like the sort of thing that would be Henry VIII's favourite fruit, but we promise you that they are worth hunting for.

DIY Ice Cream Bites

THE DISH

Making your own ice cream is essential in getting that soft and creamy middle, and this no-churn condensed milk method is the quickest (and tastiest) shortcut around. If you haven't got a large freezable container, you can set the mixture in a lined rectangular cake tin.

INGREDIENTS

600ml **double cream**
1 x 397g tin of **condensed milk**
1 tbsp **vanilla bean paste**
200g **dark chocolate**, broken into pieces
50g **salted roasted peanuts**, finely chopped
sea salt

METHOD

Put the cream, condensed milk and vanilla bean paste in a bowl and beat with an electric whisk until it forms medium peaks – it should look very thick and hold its shape like clotted cream. Transfer to a large freezable container and freeze for at least 6 hours.

When the ice cream has set, line a baking tray (that fits in your freezer) with a sheet of baking paper. Use 2 dessert spoons or a small ice cream scoop to make little balls and lay them on the baking paper. Freeze again for 15 minutes until firm to the touch.

Melt the chocolate in a heatproof bowl set over a saucepan of simmering water or in the microwave in 30-second bursts, stirring regularly, until smooth. Leave to cool.

Line another baking tray with baking paper.

Remove the ice cream from the freezer and use a fork to dunk the balls into the melted chocolate (don't worry if the base touching the fork isn't fully coated) then transfer to the lined tray. Sprinkle with the peanuts, or a pinch of flaky sea salt. Repeat with the remaining ice cream balls and work quickly!

Return the tray to the freezer for 30 minutes before enjoying. These will keep in the freezer for up to 1 month.

SWAP

Cover these in any other toppings of your choice while the chocolate is wet, like crumbled chocolate biscuits, sprinkles, different nuts or freeze-dried fruit.

TIME: 30 MINUTES + FREEZING   MAKES: 20   VEGGIE, GLUTEN-FREE

Miso Banana
Caramel Mille Feuille

THE DISH

Banoffee pie, but fancy. And only 6 ingredients. Red miso gives this dessert a handsome umami depth that'll keep you coming back for more. You can make these as individual mille feuille or bake the pastry as three big sheets and construct a big get-your-phone-out-for-a-photo dessert. Your call.

INGREDIENTS

1 sheet of **ready-rolled puff pastry**
400g **light or dark brown sugar**
525ml **double cream**
1½ tbsp **red miso**
6 ripe **bananas**, 3 roughly chopped, 3 sliced
  into rounds
100g **dark chocolate**, broken into pieces

You will need 2 piping bags.

METHOD

Preheat the oven to 210°C fan.

Roll the sheet of puff pastry out onto a baking tray, keeping it on the paper it comes with. Cut in half lengthways, then cut each half into 6 fingers, without separating them. This will give 12 individual pieces of pastry. Lay another sheet of baking paper on top of them and pop a second baking tray on top of that to act as a weight.

Put the tray into the oven for 20–22 minutes until the pastry is golden brown and perfectly crisp. Remove from the oven and allow to cool completely. Once cool, you should be able to use a serrated bread knife to separate the pieces and trim any wonky bits.

Meanwhile, set a large non-stick saucepan over a medium heat for 1 minute. Add 350g of sugar and melt gently into a caramel. This will take a few minutes – don't be tempted to pour any water in or go mad stirring it. Be patient and shake the pan now and then.

Once you have a caramel, carefully whisk in 175ml of cream and bring to a boil. It will likely seize up, but don't worry, just keep whisking until the caramel melts back down again. Reduce to a simmer and add the miso and the 3 roughly chopped bananas. Cook for 3–4 minutes, then tip into a food processor and blitz until smooth. Pop in the fridge to chill, and when cooled, add to a piping bag and set aside.

METHOD CONTINUED

Meanwhile, put the remaining cream and brown sugar in a bowl and use an electric whisk to beat it until it just reaches soft peaks. Add to a piping bag.

Melt the chocolate in a heatproof bowl set over a saucepan of simmering water or in the microwave in 30-second bursts, stirring regularly, until smooth.

To assemble the mille feuille, pipe a blob of the banana purée onto the serving plate and place a pastry finger on it to glue the base down. Now pipe a layer of the purée onto the pastry finger, top with banana slices, then pipe over some cream and drizzle over some melted chocolate. Add another pastry finger and repeat the filling process. Top with the final pastry layer, pipe over the banana purée, add more banana slices and a final drizzle of chocolate. Finish with a sprinkle of brown sugar and get stuck in.

TIP

This is a great make-ahead dessert – the caramel and cream will keep in their piping bags in the fridge for a day, and the pastry can be baked and stored in an airtight container at room temperature for a day.

Cherry Frangipane Pie

THE DISH

Your mates won't believe this is just 6 ingredients. Hell, we barely believe it's got just 6 ingredients. A sunny and summery take on the French classic of galette des rois using the season's best fruit: cherries.

INGREDIENTS

FOR THE COMPOTE
400g **fresh pitted cherries**
120g **caster sugar**

FOR THE FRANGIPANE
200g **flaked almonds**
100g **caster sugar**
140g **unsalted butter**, cold and cubed
2 large **eggs**
salt

FOR THE PASTRY
2 x 500g blocks of **puff pastry**
2 large **egg yolks**

METHOD

Start by making the poached cherry compote. Add the cherries to a large saucepan with the 120g of sugar and a splash of water. Set over a medium heat and bring to a simmer, cooking for 6–7 minutes until the cherries are tender. Scoop out the cherries with a slotted spoon and set them to one side. Continue to simmer the juice until it has reduced to a thick syrup. Stir through the cherries and allow to cool.

Meanwhile, preheat the oven to 160°C fan. Spread the flaked almonds on a baking tray in an even layer and toast in the oven for 8–10 minutes until they turn a light golden brown. Remove from the oven and allow to cool.

For the frangipane, add the toasted flaked almonds to a food processor with the 100g of sugar and a pinch of salt. Pulse until finely ground. Add the butter and pulse. Add 1 whole egg and 1 yolk. Pulse until you have a smooth, thick paste. Chill in the fridge until firm.

For the pastry, line a work surface with baking paper and roll out the first block until it is the thickness of a pound coin (you don't want it too thin!). Cut a 26cm circle out of the sheet of pastry (use a large saucepan lid as a guide to cut around if you have one). Repeat with the remaining block of pastry.

Place a disc of pastry onto a lined baking tray. Spread over the frangipane in a rough circle, leaving a 3cm border around the edge of the pastry. If the frangipane is very firm, you can mould it with your hands into a disc. Top with the cherries and just a little of the syrup. Save the rest for later.

Make an egg wash with the remaining 2 eggs by beating the yolks with a tiny splash of water. (You can freeze the egg whites for a future meringue!). Brush the pastry border with a little water. Place the other pastry disc over the top and seal around the edges with the side of your palm. Crimp with a fork or knife, egg wash the surface and then chill in the fridge for 20 minutes. Remove from the fridge and egg wash again.

Preheat the oven to 190°C fan. Cut a small hole in the top of the pie to allow any steam to escape. Decorate the pie with a light scoring pattern and cut a couple of other slits around the edge to let steam out. Return to the fridge to chill for 5–10 minutes before transferring to the preheated oven to bake for 50–55 minutes until puffed and deep golden brown in colour.

Leave to cool for 20 minutes, then slice and serve with the remaining syrup.

Index

Acknowledgements

First of all, I want to thank you for picking up this book. Without your support, Mob wouldn't be what it is today and I'm extremely thankful that you decided to purchase this in a bookshop, airport, online retailer or wherever else you might have stumbled onto *Mob 6*. This cookbook has been a real labour of love and it wouldn't have happened without the hard work of all the brilliant people behind it.

I have to start by thanking Saskia Sidey, who has been crucial in the creation of this book, from the very beginning of its journey. She's someone whose judgement and taste I hold in extremely high regard and she has been essential in turning *Mob 6* from an abstract idea into a tangible reality. Saskia was the brains behind most of the recipes within these pages, and I'm still in awe of all of the stunning dishes she has been able to create with just 6 ingredients. I am sure you will agree that the recipes in *Mob 6* look stunning, and that's all thanks to a crew of brilliant and talented individuals who assisted Saskia in the food styling department.

On top of that, I also want to give a huge shout-out to the incredible Mob Food Team, who have all contributed recipes to this book as well. Sophie Wyburd, Xiengni Zhou, Ben Lippett, Jordon King, Jodie Nixon, Angelica Udenweze and Zena Kamgaing, thank you all. You're all gems and you have done the most phenomenal job. I am so proud of the work you've done. I would also like to take this chance to thank our dedicated recipe testers for their endless honesty and appetite.

Also, a thanks to Susanna Unsworth, Immy Mucklow, Clare Cole, Connie Simons, Sophie Denmead and Beth Emmens for your assistance on the shoots, your help was invaluable!

I'll forever and always be indebted to David Loftus. David has been our photographer for the last few cookbooks and it's always a complete and utter pleasure to work with the best (and most respected) food photographer around. You've really helped bring the recipes in this book to life. Thank you also, dear Ange, for hosting us in your house for all the shoot days, and for the teas and coffees that helped us all through. You are the most welcoming, kind host. I'd be remiss not to mention David's loveable dog, Digby – an extremely good boy who never failed to brighten up everyone's day during long shoots.

Good design is an integral part of any cookbook. A cookbook needs to look beautiful. It needs to feel like a truly special object when you hold it in your hands. The design for *Mob 6* was done by the great Studio Nari. They have created something that both looks and feels stunning. Thank you for pulling out all the stops, and always going the extra mile, to ensure that this book came out as beautifully as possible. Needless to say, I think you've knocked it out of the park. Thank you also to our in-house Art Lead Joe Jarvis, who worked on the cover to get it looking just right.

Thanks to everyone on the Ebury team who helped me so much along the way. Special thanks to Emily Brickell, our ever-patient Editor – you have been the glue that has held this whole massive project together. And, of course, thank you to the greatest Publisher there is, Lizzy Gray. I have so much respect and admiration for you, and everything you do. You are truly one of a kind. Your wisdom throughout has been the guiding force that has made this book as special as it is. And I have very much enjoyed learning from you along the way.

About Mob

I couldn't get this far without giving a shout-out to the rest of the Mob team. There's so much work that goes into these books beyond just the writing of them and I'm grateful for the time and effort of everyone at Mob who has helped to make it happen. The office is a better place to be in thanks to all of you.

Lastly, I'd like to thank the people in my personal life who have helped to keep me sane throughout the creation of this book, and throughout all of the years of intense stress and joy since I started Mob. As always, thank you to Mum, Dad, Joe and Sam. I wouldn't be who I am without you. I love you all so much. Thank you. For everything.

Ben Lebus x

Mob is built around one key principle: food you'll actually cook. Mob started out as an idea – as most things do – when the company's founder, Ben, realised that barely any of his friends at university were able to cook. Armed with nothing but a kitchen, a camera and a handful of recipes, Ben started posting videos online of simple and delicious dishes that people could easily recreate at home. Mob has only gone from strength to strength since and earned a loyal and ever-growing following.

With six bestselling cookbooks already in the bag, Mob is always on the lookout for new and exciting ways to provide ambitious home cooks with the freshest recipes possible. It doesn't matter whether that's through cookbooks like this one, or on social media platforms such as Instagram, Facebook and TikTok – the Mob mission is always the same. To inspire, educate and engage with as many people as possible, connecting with them through what we love and know the most: food. Give Mob a follow to keep up to date with our latest recipes.